PRAY
BEFORE YOU
VOTE

**Jesus Is Not a Democrat or a Republican
Jesus Is Lord!**

FREYA S. HUFFMAN

Forewords By Rod P. Huffman, Brenda Fruster and Gloria Sullivan

Pray Before You Vote! by Freya S. Huffman
Copyright © 2016 by Freya S. Huffman
All Rights Reserved.
ISBN: 978-1-59755-398-8

Published by: ADVANTAGE BOOKS™
www.advbookstore.com

Unless otherwise indicated, all scripture quotations are taken from the New King James Version of the Bible, copyright © 1982 by Thomas Nelson, Inc. Used by permission.

Library of Congress Control Number: 2016941892

Cover Design by Pat Theriault

First Printing: June 2016
08 09 10 11 12 13 14 10 9 8 7 6 5 4 3 2 1
Printed in the United States of America

Dedication

This book is dedicated to my Dad, Robert Sullivan, aunt Charity Sullivan, Grandmothers Carrie Mitchell, Netha Lee Sullivan, Great Grandmother "Dear Heart Mack" whom you read about in the book, Mother Carrie Jones, Sister Lewis, Commissioner Herman Lodge, Vicki Mitchell, Carrie Mitchell, LaShonda Ward, Sonya Burgess, Ms. Freya Humphrey, Ms. Lemon, and Coach Brownlee. Mother Carrie, Paul and Glenda Vaught and Sister Lewis, you were pioneers that taught the word of God to young children throughout Waynesboro. You taught us about Jesus at a young age. Uncle Willie Tracey "Bill" Glover. Mr. Lodge, thank you for teaching us about voter's registration, politics and being passionate about civil rights. Vicki, thank you for showing us how to live life to the fullest. I miss you. LaShonda, thank you for showing us how to push through adversity and stand on faith until God calls us home. Coach thanks for recruiting me to college and giving me "second chance". You took a chance on me and you changed my life forever. I thank God for your unselfishness and commitment to developing young basketball players like me. Ms. Freya Humphrey and Ms. Esther Lemon, God used you touch a young freshman girl at Claflin University and I will always be appreciative. Carrie Mitchell, my aunt, you will always be near and dear to my heart. Although all of you have gone on to be with the Lord, you all still carry special places in my heart.

3

Freya S. Huffman

Acknowledgements

Father God, thank You for creating the heavens and the earth and everything in it. I pray that I am using the talents You have given to me to glorify Your kingdom. You knew me before I was in my mother's womb and you created me for such a time as this. I praise You and glorify You because You deserve only the best from me.

I glorify my Lord and Savior, Jesus Christ. Thank you for being my best friend. You died on the cross and was raised from the dead just for me. I appreciate you and love you. It is you who carried me through the storms and trials and it is you who interceded on my behalf to our Father in heaven. I love you and thank You for the example you have set for me.

Thank You Holy Spirit for your divine inspiration. These words came from You in the middle of the night, in the middle of the morning, while driving and sleeping. You put this word in me and I hope I am able to deliver the message You are speaking at this hour. Thank You for Your guidance.

To my husband, Rod P. Huffman: Thank you for your encouragement and your push to do and be what God has called me to be. You are a true man of God and you rightly divide the word of truth. Your message of love, hope, righteousness, integrity and God's knowledge will reach and transform the world. You will continue to slay giants and open the eyes of God's people to truth and light! You are a Pastor, Teacher, Evangelist, Motivator, Encourager, Friend and Leader. I love you and appreciate you. You are gentleman and my King! God answered my prayers when He brought you into my life.

Thank you to my children: Ryan, Ebony, Akoli, Jeremiah, Jordan, Hannah and Kendall. I appreciate you all. Thank you for your patience. You are royalty to me and God has a predestined plan for you. Seek Him diligently and follow His word. Twink thanks for laboring with me on this, you are a blessing. Your labor has not been in vain. God has great plans for your life. Also, thank you for my little inspirations: Ty, Kylie, Layla, Shelby, Raelyn, and Gabriel. Love you all much! Also, thank you Sam and the McDuffie family for taking care of my daughter and grandbabies.

Thank you Momma and Kenya, Torrance, Wes and Tori for your love, support, advice, and everything. Our lives changed forever when God brought us into the light. I would not be where I am today without the sacrifices that you two made for me. Many prophecies have been made over our lives and this is just one of many that will come to pass. I love you all and Momma, know that God will repay you for the all the sacrifices you have made for me and many others.

Thank you to my Father-in-law, Pastor- Emeritus Charles E. Huffman, Sr., Nita, Dawn, Charles (Chuck) for your love and support and accepting me into the family. Thank you and Mrs. Huffman who has gone on to be with the Lord for blessing me with your son.

To my spiritual accountability team: Rod P. Huffman Dr. Lula Hankerson, Gloria Sullivan (Mom), Uncle Sandis, Aunt Bill, Lisa, Uncle Bill, Aunt Ann, Dr. Glenn Wiggins, Sr., Pastor Brenda Fruster, and Christy. Thank you, thank you, thank you. Thank you for time, patience, honesty and clarity. You all are the greatest.

Christy, my Dare to Dream sister, thank you for introducing me to Mike and Karyn at Advantage. I pray that the seeds you have sown into me will be given backed to you 100 fold. You are a blessing!

Thanks Mike, Karyn and Pat for your patience and support. Pat, thank you for bringing the vision that God gave me to life. The book cover looks great! Thanks for the prayers and for making this dream a reality. You guys are a blessing to the body of Christ.

Special thanks to Tara, Beverly, Lisa, Ivy, Irene and Felicia, Mrs. Iris. You are true friends. You are a blessing to me. God will use you all to reach the world. Love you all.

Special thank you to my Claflin University family, you are best family ever. May God continue to bless you all in your endeavors and continue to change the world!

To Sister Lorraine, Mrs. Janice, Sis. Julia, Sis Diane, Sister Darlene, Sister Julia, Sister Jackie Free, Sister Linda Free, Sister Jackie Green Sis. Bettye, Sister Lovette, and my other sisters at Waynesboro Deliverance Church: thanks for your prayers and support. You are a rock and God will bless you for the seeds you sow into others. You are a blessing to the body of Christ and to me.

To Sister Sandra: Thanks for showing me perseverance in the midst of the storm. God is with you and He said in His word that if you abide Him, He will abide you. Ask what you will and it shall be given unto you. Walk by faith and not by sight. You have a special place in my heart.

To Vonda: Thank you for saying "it's not too late to write the book". May God bless you as you go forth in your destiny. Do not give up on your dreams because God will use you to reach women around the world!

To Pastor and Sister Wiggins: Thank you for your teaching, training and development over the last 23 years. You two have strengthened my spiritual life and allowed me to blossom in Christ. You supported my early efforts when I wanted to start a business and encouraged me to continue my education. I praise God for your ministry and the seeds you sown into me and my family. May God richly bless you. Your seeds were sown in Waynesboro and are sprouting out throughout the nation. You all really live the verse, "be fruitful and multiply". I thank God for your commitment and faithfulness to Christ. I am one of the fruits of your labor. Stand strong and continue to allow God to use you as you transform lives for Christ.

To my church family at Waynesboro Deliverance Evangelistic Church: My sisters and brothers in Christ, I thank you for your support, patience, and love throughout the years. It is here where I have grown. I love you all and praise for you. Many have poured into me and for that I will be forever grateful. You all are a blessing.

To Pastor Brenda Fruster: Pastor Brenda thank you for helping me birth my dreams. You called me a writer and you did more for me in nine months than what I could have done on my own in a lifetime. A spiritual acceleration took place when we had our brief encounter in the Dare to Dream Mentorship Program. Our nine months of intensive studying, fasting, praying and seeking placed us on God's path and not our own. You are a mighty and amazing woman of God who God will use to touch and awaken God's people around the world. May God bless you and your family.

Thank you to Mt. Zion Church, Maranatha Tabernacle, Thankful Baptist Church, Mt. Olive Church, New Life Church, Watkinsville Baptist Church and other churches in Waynesboro that I have been connected with since I was a child, God bless you.

Thank you to Rev. Rex Wright for showing us how to witness in the streets as kids with Coalition for Christ.

Thank you Coach Willie Dukes for supporting me since I was a teenager. You, Clifford Carter, Coach Robins, Coach Brown and Coach Brownlee have all poured into me to help me become who I am today.

Thank you to the Commander of the Morning Prayer team and Kimberly Daniels Ministries. You all are powerful and I thank God that I am a part of this powerful prayer team. You have pushed me in my prayer life and I praise God for your prayer and support. May God continue to rain favor upon you as you continue to rise early and declare God's word each morning!

Thank you to my aunts, uncles, cousins, family, friends and co-workers. You all have all made a difference in my life. I appreciate your encouragement and your support. May God bless you and grant you the deepest desires of your heart. Thanks to Lil Momma and Faye, I love you all.

Thank you TV49, Rejoice Radio, Gospel Alive, TBN, INSP and all Christian television, radio stations and Internet ministries for preaching the word of God. When I could not go to church because I worked so much, you became my church. Thank you.

Finally, thank you Kenneth Copeland Ministries for preaching the word of God. While watching your television broadcast about 2am in the morning, the Holy Spirit gave me the book title. You were on with David Barton. Thank you for teaching the truth of God's word.

Freya S. Huffman

Endorsements

"This book should be read by every Christian who is concerned about the leadership and direction of this country, the U.S.A. It is written by someone who is very serious about the Lord and who has a real sense of the times we live in, both politically and spiritually. Thank you Freya Huffman."

Dr. Glenn Wiggins, Sr.
Senior Pastor, Waynesboro Deliverance Evangelistic Church
Waynesboro, Georgia

"A long overdue meditation on the African American voting heritage. It immerses readers into the truth about traditional views favoring a specific political party and challenges voters to maintain a Christ-centered view/responsibility when considering who is on the ballot!"

Evangelist Christy Poindexter
Author, The 49th Year

"Freya Huffman has shared, in this book, knowledge concerning Christianity and politics that is much needed in Christendom today. Her knowledge of politics from the religious perspective is very insightful. This is a book that can be read and enjoyed while causing you to think of elections and politics in a new and exciting way! A book to be read, digested, and employed when selecting your candidates on Election Day."

Dr. Lula Hankerson
Waynesboro Deliverance Evangelistic Church

Freya S. Huffman

Table of Contents

FORWORD
by Pastor Rod P. Huffman

The proverb writer declares in Proverbs 14:34, "Righteousness exalts a nation, but sin is a reproach to any people." Here, we see living righteously (according to God's precepts) not only affects an individual, family, or a community, but ultimately, it impacts nations! Doing things God's way (called righteousness) exalts or lifts up a nation. In other words, a nation is blessed when godly leadership is in position and leads the people after the ways of the Lord. On the other hand, the scripture further declares, "sin is a reproach to any people." Another word for reproach is "a shame" or "disgrace." The definition also means one has received "a rebuke." When leaders sin by disobeying God and cause their citizens to not walk after the Lord's ways, they cause nations to be disgraced and rebuked by God. This carries with it negative consequences that can impact not only the current generation but several generations to come.

If there are three things that are made perfectly clear within the sacred scriptures of the Bible, they are: First, God is sovereign (Psalm 115:3, 2 Chronicles 20:6, Zechariah 4:6). He is all-powerful, all-present, all-knowing, and He answers to nobody but Himself. His ways are just and right, and His love for mankind (His creation) is abundant and surpasses natural understanding (John 3:16, John 15:9-13). His ways alone are right! As the Creator of everything, including mankind, He is the ultimate Ruler and Law-Giver, and it is our duty to obey and follow Him.

Second, the LORD rules in the affairs of men (Daniel 2:21, Daniel 4:17, Psalm 75:7, Isaiah 40:23). That's right, the LORD is King of kings and LORD of lords (1 Timothy 6:15, Revelation 19:16). This all-powerful, loving and just God rules in the affairs of men. In other words, it is He who places kings, rulers, presidents, etc. to serve in positions of power. It is also His choosing that removes men and women from power. No matter how powerful a ruler may be or how bad things may seem to be under the rule of evil men, the Bible teaches us that all things work according to God's ultimate plan (Genesis 50:20, Romans 8:28). God rules in the affair of men, and it is He who has the last say!

Third, it is the duty of God's people (born again believers) to be the agents of Christ seeking to fulfill His will in the earth. We are called to be ambassadors of Christ and must never forget that this earth is not our home (2 Corinthians 5:20, Hebrews 11:8-10). We are to always seek to only please the Lord and fulfill His will in our lives and in the earth (Proverbs 16:9, Isaiah 55:6-9). As partners with God to assert godly influence within the earth, the people of God have a mandate to act! We can't idly sit on the sidelines and simply "hope" and "wish" that godly leaders will be elected. We must act! We must declare "Kingdom of God come, will of God be done!" and do what we can (being led of God's Spirit) to elect leadership that will seek after the LORD. As dual citizens in heaven and earth, we must vote!

Fourth, since we are earthly creatures and the Lord abides in heaven, the only way we can ensure we are carrying out heaven's mandate is to receive our directions from heaven. One of the ways God gives direction to His people is through His Word, the Holy Bible. The Word of God spells out what God's will is for His creation...it reveals to us the mind and heart of God. In addition to the Word of God, another way we receive these directions or orders from heaven's headquarters is through a spiritual and effective medium called "Prayer!" (Matthew 6:10, 1 Timothy 2:1-3). On the surface, prayer is simply one communicating with God. Prayer is one talking to God and then pausing and listening to see what the LORD is speaking back to him. If we are to cast our vote in alignment with God's will, we must seek His face in prayer!

In this impactful book, Freya Huffman emphasizes the importance of God's people praying so they may discern which candidates deserve their vote...that is, the vote that is cast for the candidate that best represents God's values. Without bias, she not only explains the reasons it's important to pray before one votes, but she also gives a great litmus test for one to consider when trying to vote for a candidate that values God's will and ways. Filled with great insight and meaningful prayer guides, "Pray Before You Vote!" is a book that every citizen must have in their collection. I highly recommend this literary piece and have no doubt that you (the reader) will benefit from its contents.

Rodney P. Huffman

Founder, New Destiny Community Church, Cocoa, FL & Rod Huffman Evangelistic Ministries, International (RHEMI), Warner Robins, GA

Freya S. Huffman

FORWORD
by Pastor Brenda Fruster

Whether or not you spend a portion of your life studying the ins and outs of politics and its fearless leaders, your life is undeniably affected by the various political affairs that run our country. As Christians, our one true leader is Jesus Christ, therefore the way we live our lives is governed first by the Word of God. Nevertheless, the Word of God instructs us to work and pray for the good of the country where we live and that if it prospers, we too shall prosper.

Also, seek the peace and prosperity of the city to which I have carried you into exile. Pray to the LORD for it, because if it prospers, you too will prosper. (Jeremiah 29:7, NIV)

Freya Huffman examines the various ways in which political parties strive to work for the good of the country, according to the belief system of the various parties. Her years of interest, study, and prayer in the area of politics comes alive in this book as she explores the importance of voting, the mixing of politics and religion, and the motivation behind voting preferences of the African-American culture.

As a former student of my *Dare to Dream Mentorship* class, Freya is a woman after God's own heart. She is a true woman of God with a heart for our nation and the politics that govern it. As you read on, I know her words will inspire you to take action in the political arena as she demonstrates the importance of the Christian vote!

Brenda Fruster
Co-Pastor Kingdom Worship Center
Tampa, Florida

Freya S. Huffman

FORWORD
BY Gloria Sullivan, Mom

This book is an eye-opener and it can be used as a voting manual. Always pray before you vote and use your vote to stand up and help make a difference in your community. The word of God says that you will know them, the candidates, by their fruit. It is important to know each candidate and know who you are putting in office. In this book you will get a lot of information to help you because it is full of meat and the word. Some may have difficulty in digesting it, but take time to read it, chew a little at a time until you can digest it.

This is a challenge to see what we can do as kingdom citizens of the United States to make a difference in our country. We need to have intelligent conversations based on the word of God. Take time to listen to the audible voice of God. When you hear God's voice always obey it. Wait on God to speak to you so He can tell you who to vote for. You can make a difference and in order to make a difference at the polls, you must be a registered voter. The next step is to gather information on each candidate and know what each candidate stands for. Sometimes you may have to call around to get information on the candidate. Know their platform. The next step is to pray, then go to the polls and vote. We all have a right to vote. It is time to take advantage of this voting rights process.

You need to know what is going on in your community. You can stand together as a kingdom citizen to make a difference in your community. Know the issues in your community and take a look at the way the candidates have been voting in the past. It is time for you to take the time to be informed on the issues and make a difference at the polls. It is time for us to open our eyes up to the truth. In this voting process, be encouraged to vote and do not be afraid. It is your God-given right to stand up and vote. Go to the polls with a clear heart. Keep your mind fixed on God. You can make a difference by doing the right thing. There are some agency personnel who provide voter registration services for any applicant to register to vote. It is time to rise up and be counted and your time is now. Before you go to the polls, acknowledge God in all that you do. Let God direct your footsteps and you cannot go wrong.

It is time for a change from things the same old way. We have to consider what the Lord would want us to do. We have to ask God for wisdom in each situation. It can be done if we trust God. A mind is a terrible thing to waste, a vote is a terrible thing to waste and leaving Christ out of your life is a terrible thing to waste.

I have known Freya all of her life. She always had others on her heart. She always wanted to help make a difference in the community before the age of ten years old. She gave her life to the Lord at the age of five. She and her sister walked door to door passing out voter education information. This time the Lord has elevated her to a higher level in writing this book. We know the readers will be blessed by reading it. Freya is a Kingdom woman of God. She loves the Lord and she loves people. This book was birthed into her by the Holy Spirit. The Word of God says "my sheep hear my voice and my stranger they will not follow". As the Holy Spirit continued to lead and guide her, she continued to write. I commend Freya for writing this book. I stand with her because she spent a lot of prayerful time and research on writing this book. Freya is a woman of God with a humble spirit. She listens for that still small voice of God. She is very passionate about her work and she gives all honor and glory to God.

We all should pray before we vote and acknowledge God. This is only wisdom when we do so. God always knows more about each candidate or situation. The time is out for just putting people in office and we do not know what they stand for. If a candidate stands for something that is against God's word and we vote for them anyway, I believe the blood of Jesus will be on our hands.

It is time for kingdom citizens to wake up. If the candidates are elected, they will make decisions concerning our city, county, state and country and decisions about you. This is why it is important to pray before you vote knowing that Jesus is in control. Jesus is Lord! God gave us a will and we have a choice, but God will not lord over you. Take time to pray and let the Lord lead you, then vote and be proud to be an American to stand up for what is right. Use your God-given power. Wake up America! Pray! Vote! It is now or never. When you pray, you will hear God's voice. We must obey God when He speaks. God's ways and thinking are not like ours. You must choose this day whom you will serve. You have a comforter, the Holy Spirit, and when you acknowledge Him, you cannot go wrong. There is a wealth of information in this book. It is time to take a serious look at voting and the candidates.

When reading this book, the Lord may give you more to add. Let it be used to discuss issues in a positive way. This is book is about the past, present and what we can do to improve the future as we vote.

I believe this book is anointed by God because she wrote it as the Holy Spirit gave it to her. Freya is very passionate about her work and she gives all honor and glory to God.

Make sure everyone in your household, on your street, on your job and in your church are registered voters. Encourage them to pray, do their homework on the candidates and vote on election day. You can vote by absentee ballot also. Check to see if there is early voting in your community. Foremost pray and stand up, be counted and make a difference in your community.

Gloria Sullivan, Mom

Freya S. Huffman

Prologue

The Awakening

I have been involved in politics since I was a young girl. My mom, my sister and I would pass out voter's registration material leading up to every local, state and national election. We would get flyers and go door-to-door informing people about their right to vote and why our candidate should get their vote. Many people would say "I was not going to vote, but if these little girls can get out here and campaign, I can get out and vote!"

Many people become loyal to a political party because of their shared beliefs. People have a desire to belong. It is human nature for people to belong. Clubs and organizations are founded by people who have similar interests every day. Sometimes, the overall view of organization is not the view of all, but people are still part of the organization. When we become part of the body of Christ, our views should reflect God's views. We are commanded to take up His cross and follow Him. His cross represents His values and His standard.

About nine months prior to the 2004 Presidential election, the Holy Spirit put this topic in my heart:
I am Not A Democrat!
I am Not A Republican!
I am a Christian!"
Once the Holy Spirit dropped this in my spirit, my focus was the beginning to shift to God's views instead of my own. The Holy Spirit lives in us and He knows the mind of God. When He speaks to us and we know it is Him speaking to us, He is speaking what God is speaking. In my case, He was prompting me to adjust my

ways to God's ways. The Word of God says His ways are not our ways and His thoughts are not our thoughts (Isaiah 55:8). When we become Christians, we become new creatures in Christ Jesus and old things are passed away and all things become new. Our old nature is just that, old. We identify with Christ now and there is an adjusting that has to take place. We have a new DNA. Our DNA mirrors Christ.

The purpose of this book is to share my eye-opening revelation about the morality of voting and the importance of praying before voting. I was watching Kenneth Copeland on television early one morning and David Barton was his guest. David Barton said something that caught me off guard. He said that historically the Republicans were the ones who fought for civil rights and fought to abolish slavery. I thought that if I am a Christian and they are Christians, I need to at least check the facts and see the history of the parties. I could not believe my ears. Could this really be true? This is a man of God who is saying that Republicans were for African-American people. I wanted to find out if this was really true. I wanted to learn more about the history of the political parties and why there is division. This started my curiosity about the two major parties and their views. I started my research to find out about the history of the parties because today it seems the Democrats are for the underrepresented people. The Republicans seemed to care about morality and corporate America. What changed in the last 100 years? The Holy Spirit led me to write a book about Christ's values not a party's values. Why did the political parties split? Why did the Democratic party take on the mantle of mercy and justice for all people? Why does the Republican party seem to carry the morality mantle? Both of these qualities represent Christ. One group seems to support some views of Christ while the other group supports the other views of Christ. How did the parties evolve to what they are today? How do we,

Christian Democrats, Christian Republicans and Christian Independents, become unified in the Word of God? As I began writing the book, I realized the focus should be on Jesus' ways, not our personal views. This prompted the need to include Jesus in the subtitle. This topic alone should have given me some insight that the winners of the election would be people who professed Christ openly and who were not afraid to share it. My vote was not based on my party affiliation but as the Holy Spirit led me. I heard an inner voice but I was still not certain about the candidates, especially the Presidential candidates of 2004. Both (George W. Bush and John Kerry) said they believed in God and both seemed like they cared about the people, still I was torn. So, my journey began to determine which was a better candidate for the job. I prayed the night before and the Holy Spirit spoke clearly to me and said, "vote for the one that prays to me daily". I interpreted this to mean, seek the one who seeks the face of God daily. Both men seemed like God-fearing men. One carried the morality mantle and the other carried the social issues mantle. I was not sure.

I began to see African-American Republicans run for office. Herman Cain, ran for senator on the Republican ticket for the state of Georgia. I was a fan because of his guest appearance on the Chicago-based Black entrepreneur show on which he shared words of wisdom for entrepreneurs. I watched him faithfully every Saturday morning at 7:00 AM. When I saw that he was running for the Republican ticket, it took me back again. I was a big fan of his and he had been very successful. I met him when he was a guest speaker for an entrepreneurship event in Augusta, Georgia at a local campaign event. I even shared my title with him and he found it interesting. I saw God using Christians from both parties who were from different racial backgrounds. God was changing the political outlook. People were not afraid to declare that "Jesus is

Lord" in their campaigns. There was a boldness for Christ bursting through that had been hidden for so long because of the fear of rejection. Also, pioneers such as Reverend Al Sharpton have led the forefront on Civil Rights and justice for all people. He cared about how people are treated and he also professes Christ.

As you read this book, you will travel the road of discovery with me. I will attempt to answer questions you may have regarding the impact of your vote, Christ's values, mixing religion and politics, and if and how Jesus would have voted! My goal is to challenge the Christian Democrat, Republican, Independent and every other type of Christian party affiliate to look beyond the party. We must look to the Holy Spirit for guidance and wisdom in our decision-making.

This book is written to the people who have the compassion of Christ who follow God's word, the people who care about the poor and the needy, the people who stand up for injustice and against immorality. The Holy Spirit has come to guide us into all truth. John 14:17 tells us *"the Spirit of truth, whom the world cannot receive, because it neither sees Him nor knows Him; but you know Him, for He dwells with you and will be in you"*. If you are a Christian, then you should be open to the scripture for it is what we live by. This book's focus is not to endorse one party over another nor is this a denunciation of the political structure as it exists today, unless God leads us to. It is to endorse Christ and our allegiance to Him first and foremost before our allegiance to our personal interests, race, gender, cultural background or political party. Christ has given us all the ministry of reconciliation to Him first and then to each other (2nd Corinthians 5:18 – 20). God is calling for unity among Christendom regardless of our political party affiliation. Will we stand up for Christ's values and listen to the Holy Spirit as He guides us into all truth? Or will we be a people who continues to conform to the world and its popularity?

God is calling us from behind our political curtains so the spotlight of the Holy Ghost will shine upon His people. It is curtain call for God's people. It is time to audition and distinguish the real from the fake, the weak from the strong and truth from deception.

Christians are you are you ready? We are the light of the world. We are to shine in the midst of darkness! Please be open-minded and look deep within yourself as we take this journey together, pray before you vote!

Freya S. Huffman

Introduction

Jesus is Not a Democrat or a Republican!

Jesus came to the earth to save the world. He chose twelve men of diverse backgrounds and taught them truth so they could teach others. These men had different views but once they had an encounter with Jesus, their minds were renewed. Jesus used them despite of their backgrounds. To say Jesus was a Republican or a Democrat would limit Jesus' ability to reach all, teach all, heal all, and love all. We would limit His ability to reach the murderers, the poor, the prisoners, the prostitutes, the homosexuals, the lesbians, the liars and the thieves. We would deny the very essence of His being. We know that in His time here on earth, there were no Democrats or Republicans but rather there were Pharisees and Sadducees. Jesus often disagreed with their way of government and their views. He often pointed out their self-righteous attitudes and exposed them when they questioned him about issues such as taxes, marriage, divorce and the resurrection (Matthew 19 and 22). They embraced religion more than they embraced Him. They missed the coming of the Messiah, because their religious traditions were more important than serving Jesus. They wanted to challenge Him at each opportunity because it was blasphemous for to them to accept Jesus Christ. Their focus was on Abraham and Moses. Jesus did not fit the description of "their" Messiah. This proves that their truths were not God's truth. Their inability to receive Him as Messiah did not change the fact that He was the Messiah. Our inability to receive God's word as law does not change the fact that His word is true. For example, if I did not believe in gravity and I jumped from a building, what would happen? The law of gravity would prove true because my weight is heavier than the air. It would be a tragic sight because I did not believe in gravity, although the law gravity is true. The same holds true with God's word. When we reject God's word, it does not mean that it is not true. **Romans 3:3** states it plainly, *"For what if some did not believe? Will their unbelief make the faithfulness of God without effect?"* Just because you do not believe, it does not change the word of God. His Word is still effective and it is still true!

As a Christian, a follower of Christ, know whom you serve and always be ready to say why you believe what you believe.

1 Timothy 3:16 tells us the Great Mystery and who Jesus is.

And without controversy great is the mystery of godliness: God was manifested in the flesh, Justified in the Spirit, Seen by angels, Preached among the Gentiles, Believed on in the world, Received up in glory. (NKJV)

John 1:1-2 further proves who Jesus is.

In the beginning was the Word, and the Word was with God, and the Word was God. He was with God in the beginning.

Our Lord and Savior, Jesus Christ, is not the same as Allah, or Baal, or Scientology, or any other God. He is the only true, supreme, holy, righteous God. He has all power: power to heal, power to deliver and power to set the captives free. John 14:6, tells us, He is the way, the truth and the life. He is the only way to Heaven. While others might die for their God, our God died for us. He is supreme! He is excellent! He is almighty! We must know this without a shout of a doubt! We must never equate Him to anyone. Paul warned Timothy *"to teach no other doctrine, nor give heed to fables and endless genealogies, which cause disputes rather than godly edification which is in faith" (1 Timothy 1:4).*

He even said if an angel comes with another gospel, we are not to accept it either. Proverbs 30 tells us that we are not to add any words to the gospel. We are to only preach the gospel of Jesus Christ and be ready to explain why we believe what we believe. Teaching another gospel and calling it God's is denying the very power of Jesus and is denying the faith.

One example of embracing another doctrine can be seen with the release of The Davinci code. This movie portrays Jesus as being married to Mary Magdalene. Christians are reading this and questioning their faith. Know the Word of God. Know whom you serve and do not doubt what you know is true. Do not preach or accept any other gospel except Jesus Christ. Jesus was born of the Virgin Mary through the Immaculate Conception. Man was not involved. Joseph was His natural father but the Holy Spirit impregnated Mary.

God is Holy. Holy by definition means sanctified and set a part. God is sinless and He sent His Son who committed no sin as a sacrifice for His people. That is love! *"God so loved the world that He gave His only begotten Son and whoever believes in Him should not perish but have everlasting life"* (John 3:16). What is everlasting life? This is eternal life with God in heaven forever. This means never being separated from God. When you have not accepted Him, you are separated from Him and this means you are in eternal darkness.

We cannot think we know who He is. We have to know who He is in order to spread the Gospel. We must be careful to stay true to the Word of God and make sure we know whom we serve. We cannot limit Jesus to one party. He can reach across party lines. He is the way of salvation, the prince of Peace and King of Kings and Lord of Lords!

John 10:11, He tells us **Jesus is the true Shepard.** In verse 5, He tells us *"His sheep know His voice and a stranger they will not* *follow"*. **Jesus is the Good Shepard.** "The good shepherd gives His life for the sheep." **The Shepard knows His sheep.** Jesus says in John 10:27-30 *"My sheep hear My voice, and I know them, and they follow Me. And I give them eternal life, and they shall never perish; neither shall anyone snatch them out of My hand. My Father, who has given them to Me, is greater than all; and no one is able to snatch them out of My Father's hand. I and My Father are one."*

Jesus is holy and worthy to be praised. His ways are not our ways and His thoughts are not our thoughts. His political structure is not of this world. He lived by the word of God and He IS the Word of God. During Jesus' time on earth He walked, talked and reached out to people. He encouraged people and awakened people to the truth of God's word and who He was. He would encourage us to judge a man by his fruit.

We have been called to be ambassadors of Christ which means we represent Christ. Many Christians are misrepresenting Christ and His gospel, Christianity. We have been hypocritical with our words and our actions. We have become extreme left and extreme right in our views by pushing our own agendas instead of Gods'. We have been double-minded in our ways. We have neglected the poor, needy, homeless, widows, fatherless and motherless. We have allowed injustice to prevail and have pushed war instead of peace. We have turned our backs to the Bible and allowed the world to legislate laws without our input. We have neglected the country through the lack of prayer. We have turned our heads to nations where people are hungry and people who are being slaughtered by the thousands everyday.

We have removed God from our schools and we have allowed Satan to come in and take over. We have allowed children to kill children and mothers to kill babies. We have neglected to enforce child labor laws and protect women and young girls from prostitution, barbaric acts and abuse. We have turned our heads because it is not in our backyard. We have allowed gangs to take over neighborhoods of the innocent and elderly. School shootings have become the norm. Terrorist plots have become the norm. We have been silent for too long.

Our political parties are deadlocked and cannot unify to pass laws to govern the nation and protect the people of this nation. They are running the government their way instead of God's way.

It is time to put down our mantle and pick up the mantle of Jesus Christ. We can pick it up when we vote! Allow the Holy Spirit to guide you and trust His word. He will never lead you the wrong way. He will guide you into all truth. Your vote will make a difference regardless of what the outcome may be.

Jesus used His voice to speak about the things of God and we should too! He did not attach Himself to one group of people. He worked with people from all walks of life. He got involved to change their lives for the better. He set the example. Will you follow Him? In Romans 12:12, Paul tells us *"we are to be transformed by the renewing of our mind that we may prove what is the good and acceptable and the perfect will of God"*.

Jesus came to earth and lived an example that we could follow. He stressed the importance of justice, mercy and peace. In the book of Isaiah, it was prophesied that the government would be upon His shoulders and His name would be called: wonderful, counselor, the mighty God, the everlasting father and the prince of peace. Seek His face, get involved and pray before you vote!

There is one body and one Spirit, just as you were called in one hope of your calling; one Lord, one faith, one baptism; one God and Father of all, who is above all, and through all, and in you all. (Ephesians 4:4-6)

Freya S. Huffman

Chapter One

Should My Vote Be Based On A Political Party?

All the ways of man are clean in his own eyes; but the Lord weigheth the spirits (Proverbs 16:2).

My allegiance has always been to my political party since I was a young girl. Most of my views like many others have been shaped by my environment and my background. We grew up in a community that was predominately African-American. We would campaign for our favorite local and national candidates whose views were similar to our views. In my teenage years, our family went through a transition. We joined a spirit-filled church and many of the beliefs and allegiances that we formed were being challenged. While we joined the church and got baptized at this old church, this new atmosphere was challenging us to know God in a more intimate way. Our belief system was being challenged. Our allegiance was not to our political party or our race, but it was shifting to God. God is the creator of all and when we accepted Jesus as our personal savior, our personal views had to be put aside and become aligned with Jesus.

We had to adopt the Word of God as our guide and adjust our personal beliefs to God's ways. Yes, we would still speak out against injustice. Yes, we would still help those who were unfortunate, but we had to first seek and trust God for wisdom and guidance instead of depending on our ideals. My allegiance was to my race, because I am an African-American. I would further go on to say that my allegiance has been to my gender, because I am a woman. I am a woman who is African-American and who grew up being very loyal to the Democratic party. Why this loyalty you may ask? I am a product of my environment. I grew up Black in the South and growing up Black in the south had its challenges. I saw racism and prejudice first hand and I still see it today. I saw discrepancies and injustice with my own eyes. When someone comes along and gives you a beacon of hope and shows care and concern about your well being even though you are Black in the South, even though you are a woman and even though you are poor, you become loyal and you form an allegiance. Others may have reasons for being loyal to their party but my loyalty rose from someone standing in the face of racism, in the face of poverty and in the face of injustice. Some are loyal because their parents, grandparents or great-grandparents were affiliated with a political party. My party cared about common people like myself. So the overall view of the Democratic party to me was to stand against racism, injustice, poverty and the Party provided a level playing field for all people. Many of the Democrats I know are born-again Christians. Then I began to meet Christians who were Republicans. This was an eye-opener. Their allegiance was to God also. Therefore if there are Christian Democrats, Christian Republicans and Christian Independents, then what party should I be a part of?

Should our vote be based on a political party? Paul tells us in Philippians 3:20 - 21 *"For our citizenship is in heaven, from which we also eagerly wait for the Savior, the Lord Jesus Christ, who will transform our lowly body that it may be conformed to His glorious body, according to the working by which He is able even to subdue all things to Himself."* This alone confirms that we should be looking to Christ as our guide. The Christians' citizenship is in heaven, nor on earth. We should mirror heaven's setup. In Miles

Monroe's book, Kingdom Principles, he discusses in detail how we are to live as if it were in the Kingdom of Heaven. We are in this world, not of this world.

Christians are becoming more vocal about issues they deem important. They are using their voice as their vote to speak up for their beliefs. As we become more vocal about our beliefs we must be sure to pray and seek God in our decision-making. When supporting a political party, we must ask questions to see if the party is bearing Christ-like fruit. What is the foundation of the political party? Was the party built on God's principles? Is the party following the principles of Jesus today? After asking these questions, we have to continue to test the spirit to see if it is aligning with the Word of God. John 1:4 warns us not to *"believe every spirit, but test the spirits to see whether they are from God, because many false prophets have gone out into the world"*. While the root is holy, the branches should be holy but some branches can be broken off because they can become contaminated. When a portion of something becomes contaminated it destroys the entire product. Solomon tells us that "the little foxes spoil the vine" (Song of Solomon 2:15). The true root should be Jesus Christ. The branches are us, His children. When something is broken from its root, it is dead. There are many who came to Christ, accepted Him and who later turned away. They are not walking with Him today. They have become contaminated and are now dead to Christ. Trees are known by their fruit and when a tree branch falls to the ground, it no longer has life. It is not fruitful. It can not produce anything. This is affirmed in John 15:1-7 where Jesus says:

> *I am the true vine, and my Father is the gardener. He cuts off every branch in me that bears no fruit, while every branch that does bear fruit he prunes (clips, cuts, shave) so that it will be even more fruitful. You are already clean because of the word I have spoken to you.*

Remain in me, and I will remain in you. No branch can bear fruit by itself; it must remain in the vine. Neither can you bear fruit unless you remain in me. I am the vine; you are the branches. If a man remains in me and I in him, he will bear much fruit; apart from me you can do nothing. If anyone does not remain in me, he is like a branch that is thrown away and withers; such branches are picked up, thrown into the fire and burned. If you remain in me and my words remain in you, ask whatever you wish, and it will be given you. This is to my Father's glory, that you bear much fruit, showing yourselves to be my disciples.

You cannot be productive if you are dead. If you remain in Jesus, you will bear much fruit and without him you cannot do anything. If you do not remain in Jesus, you are like a branch that is thrown away. You must see if the political party is part of the root which is Jesus. Remember Jesus said in 1 John 5:17 that apart from God he can do nothing. That same truth applies to us also. Apart from God we can do nothing. If we do anything apart from God, it is from the flesh. Anything done in the flesh produces no fruit.

Are you still a part of the root? If your party was founded on the Godly principles, are you still holding true to the Word of God today? I am not talking about preaching one part of the gospel and leaving out the other. I am talking about preaching the entire gospel. Are you a withered branch that is attached to the true vine but are really unfruitful and dead? What are the branches? The branches are the members of the church body, the President, the members of the Congress, the members of the Senate and the government. Are you attached to the true vine or are you are withered branch?

America was built on Christian values but are all American's Christians? No, of course not. Therefore, we cannot expect all members of a party to be Christians or accept Christ's values either. We have broken branches and limbs that are detached from the vine and they are dead to Christ! How do you check to see if a branch is dead or alive? We have to check their fruit. Galatians 5:22 states *"the fruit of the Spirit are love, joy, peace, patience, kindness, goodness, faithfulness, gentleness and self-control"*. Do the candidates possess these qualities?

We also have to check to see what the candidate believes. Does the candidate believe that Jesus is the son of God? Has the candidate confessed with their mouth that they are saved and have they repented of their sins? If so, then the root is holy. Now let us test the branches. Are the branches fruitful? Is the candidate living out the Word of God? Does the candidate have the mind of Christ? Does the candidate possess the love of Christ? Does the candidate put this love into action? If the answer to these questions is yes, then there is a pretty good chance that this branch is fruitful and it is attached to the true vine, Jesus. We must still continue to test the spirit to see if they are truly of God. If they are not showing the love of Christ in their actions or if they do not possess the qualities of Christ in their decision-making, then there is a chance that this branch is detached and therefore unfruitful. This is why prayer is key in our decision-making. While we look at the external, God examines the heart. All we have to go by is external but with the guidance of the Holy Spirit, He will guide us into all truth. We cannot judge a man's heart but we can judge a man's actions.

In terms of voting, the action of the candidate is the way they vote on issues that are presented before them. Each Christian candidate should desire the wisdom of God. When God asked Solomon what he desired, Solomon could have asked for money, materials things or even long life. Instead he asked for wisdom.

With this wisdom Solomon was able to make wise decisions even without knowing all the details. Mike Murdock is like Solomon of today and he his entire ministry is focused on sharing the wisdom of God. We need to learn to hear the voice of God and not our own voice or agenda. An example of Solomon's wisdom can be seen in 1 Kings 3:16-28 where two unmarried women came before him to lay claim to a child.

Now two women who were harlots came to the king, and stood before him. And one woman said, "O my lord, this woman and I dwell in the same house; and I gave birth while she was in the house. Then it happened, the third day after I had given birth, that this woman also gave birth. And we were together; no one was with us in the house, except the two of us in the house.

And this woman's son died in the night, because she lay on him. So she arose in the middle of the night and took my son from my side, while your maidservant slept, and laid him in her bosom, and laid her dead child in my bosom. And when I rose in the morning to nurse my son, there he was, dead. But when I had examined him in the morning, indeed, he was not my son whom I had borne."

Then the other woman said, "No! But the living one is my son, and the dead one is your son." And the first woman said, "No! But the dead one is your son, and the living one is my son." Thus they spoke before the king. And the king said, "The one says, 'This is my son, who lives, and your son is the dead one'; and the other says, 'No! But your son is the dead one, and my son is the living one.'|"

Then the king said, "Bring me a sword." So they brought a sword before the king. And the king said, "Divide the living child in two, and give half to one, and half to the other." Then the woman whose son was living spoke to the king, for she yearned with compassion for her son; and she said, "O my lord, give her the living child, and by no means kill him!" But the other said, "Let him be neither mine nor yours, but divide him."

So the king answered and said, "Give the first woman the living child, and by no means kill him; she is his mother." And all Israel heard of the judgment which the king had rendered; and they feared the king, for they saw that the wisdom of God was in him to administer justice.

Solomon used his wise judgment to determine the maternity of the child. When he requested his sword to divide the child in two, the real mother said *"O my lord, give her the living child, and by no means kill him!"* The mother whose child was dead said *"Let him be neither mine nor yours, but divide him."* How would he know who was telling the truth except by relying on the wisdom of God? This is the same wisdom he asked for when God appeared to him at Gideon. *"God appeared to him in a dream by night and said "Ask! What shall I give you?" And Solomon said "You have shown great mercy to Your servant David my father, because he walked before You in truth, in righteousness, and in uprightness of heart of with You; You have continued this kindness to him, and You have given him a son to sit on the throne, as it is this day."* (1 Kings 3:5-6). Solomon did not rely on his on judgment but he asked for the wisdom of God and as a result, he ruled with fairness and righteousness.

Check the Voting Record

We need God's wisdom in our vote and our decision-making. Should our vote be based on a political party? What is the view of the party? What are the views of the individual branches? If the root is Jesus Christ, then it will never become contaminated. While the root is holy and cannot be contaminated, the branches can be and are thus broken off or detached from God. To take it a step further it also means looking at the individuals that are running for office and their voting record. During the 2004 Presidential election, there was an assumption that voting Republican was morally right and voting Democrat was morally wrong. This theme seemed to resonate in the churches. While there are Republicans that profess Christianity, there are also just as many Democrats that profess Christianity. The perception is that Republicans are seen closer to the moral line than Democrats. It seems that Republicans are willing to broadcast their views and put laws in place to support those views. The Democrats generally believe that it is your choice. Broadcasting these views alone is not the only indication of Christianity, but putting these views into action is the ultimate proof. The Democrats generally do not legislate morality. Jesus told us that if we profess Christ before men, He will profess us before our Father but if we deny Him before men, He will deny us before our Father. (Matthew 10:33). We should profess Christ before men and we must be sure that we are living a life of Christ along with this profession.

Looking at the candidates in 2016, Donald Trump is leading the Republican Party by winning many of the primaries and Hillary Clinton is leading the Democratic party at the time of printing. While Donald Trump is representing the Republican Party, the Republican Party is divided. They are not pleased with him being the front runner. He does not represent the Party's conservative views. He won against Ted Cruz, Marco Rubio, and Ben Carson although these candidates are more conservative and represent moral views. This proves the Republican Party is not a Christian party only and others that are not Christians are voting for Donald Trump. What this does reveal is that there is a difference in views within the Party otherwise Donald Trump would not have made it this far. Christians should not just align themselves with this party because of the name, Republican however align with the values of Jesus' Christ.

If we look at the platforms of the Republicans and the Democrats, we can see where the focus is. Democrats embrace all people and generally do not think that politics and morals should mix. They generally feel that morality is a person's free will and morality should not be legislated. Republicans are not afraid to legislate morality and one such example is abortion. Republicans believe a law should be in place to prevent abortion. There are many Democrats that do not believe in abortion but they believe in a woman's right to choose. After all God gave us a free will to accept Him or reject Him. Should we have a free will to do with our bodies as we please? 1 Corinthians 6:19 tells us that ***"Do you not know that your body is a temple (dwelling place, house of God, cathedral, place of worship) of the Holy Spirit who is in you, whom you have from God, and you are not your own?)"***. When you accept Christ as your personal savior, you are not your own. You are to submit to Christ and His ways and you will come under the submission of the Holy Spirit. If you are not of Christ this makes no sense to you. (1 Corinthians 2:14). You are really not of Christ and these things are foolishness to you. God gives life and man should not take it away. We don't accept someone murdering another person; why should we take a life through abortion? This is something to think about.

We should not limit God and allow one issue to be the deciding factor. Many think that abortion is the only deciding issue in terms of voting, the moral litmus test. While this is vitally important, other issues are as important such as justice for all people, taking care of the poor, domestic violence and protecting children. God says all have sin and there is no sin greater and that all have sinned no one is righteous on his own. We must be careful and not obtain a self-righteous spirit and think that our political party is better than another like the Pharisees thought they were better. God weighs the spirits of the man (John 16:13). Democrats believe in world peace and are against wars but Republicans generally support wars. Jesus said that He is the prince of peace. Also, we find instances in the Bible where war was necessary. Even today, we have a military so we can be ready to defend ourselves from intruders of our land such as terrorists or anyone who would try to take our democracy.

Many of our leaders, Martin Luther King, Jr. along with leaders such Dr. A. H. Hoffman, *my husband's grandfather,* Representative John Lewis, Andrew Young, Rev. Jessie Jackson spear-headed the non-violence movement. In the face of adversity, racism, and death, Dr. Martin Luther King stood against war and violence. Our beloved, Mrs. Coretta Scott King continued the mission with the King Center and impacted the world with the non-violence movement. The mantle has now been passed on to Rev. Bernice King, the daughter of Dr. Martin Luther King, Jr. and Mrs. Coretta Scott King. In Rev. Bernice King's tribute to Mrs. Coretta Scott King during her home going service, she said that "We need a new birth. We have moved away from God's original intent and we have settled." She continued on to say if we had continued to embrace this non-violence movement today, I believe we could have affected the world by being an example". During this exceptional tribute to Mrs. Coretta Scott King during her home going service, four United States Presidents joined in paying their respects: Two Republicans (George Bush Sr. and George W. Bush) and Two Democrats (Jimmy Carter and William Jefferson Clinton). God use Rev.

Bernice King to tie it all together. It was not by accident or chance that all of these pioneers of Civil Rights Movement and Presidents assembled at a church called New Birth. It was divine order. God had a strategic plan to release this word to the nations so our allegiance would return to Christ. Rev. Bernice King expressed it appropriately when she stated that "God wanted us to be born again. He wants us born to Him and we need to get it right."

Instead we have pushed our own agenda ahead of God's and then we want God to bless it. When we do this, we are out of order. Even in the church today, we are doing many things that is part of our agenda we are out of order. We want to set up the order of service without consulting the Holy Spirit and we want God to bless it. We make decisions and ask God to bless without consulting Him first. We should consult the Holy Spirit in every aspect of our lives, including voting.

Voting is very important because it allows us to set the laws of the land. Where we must be careful is voting based on loyalty to a political party. Since there are flaws in both parties, being affiliated with a party does not make you more moral than another especially if you are not personally applying those morals. Just as being a member of a certain church does not make you more holy or righteous than someone else. For example, if the Democrat party supports taking care of the poor and needy but a Democratic candidate does not support this, should we vote for this person? On the other side, if the Republican Party's stance is we are against abortion and a Republican candidate says that he is for abortion, should we vote for that candidate? We must be careful not to associate one candidate with the entire organization. Remember the branches can become withered and therefore unfruitful. This is why all branches must be tested to see if they have become detached from the vine. All these issues are important and we have to pray and seek God on what He wants us to do.

There are many Republicans whose views do not align with the word of God but many people feel they should vote for the candidate because they are on the Republican ticket. There are many Democrats whose views do not align with the word of God also and many people feel they should vote for them out of loyalty. God challenges us to watch wolves in sheep's clothing and this is within both parties. There have been many examples of candidates joining a political party and once they are voted in, they switch parties. This is deceptive because many people chose to vote for the candidate because of their party affiliation. This is an example of why we should establish our views on the Word of God and not a political party. God told us to be wise as serpents and harmless as doves (Matthew 10:16). We should not be deceived if we are walking in the spirit. The Bible tells us to be wise as a serpent and innocent as a dove. We are to be wise, sharp, keen to the devices of the enemy. A dove is innocent and blameless. It represents purity and holiness. As people of God, we should mirror the characteristics of a dove.

If we were to become sensitive to the Holy Spirit and seek His guidance in our vote, He will guide us into all truth, God's truth. **John 16:13 reminds us that He is the Spirit of truth who will guide us into all truth.** God speaks through His prophets and we must pray and seek God in our decision-making. By doing this we know we are seeking God's counsel instead of man's.

Prayerfully consider your candidate because the Holy Spirit will give you discernment on who you should vote for. God will lead you in the right direction if you trust Him.

Growing Morally Questions
Have I voted based on a political party in the past?
Do I vote because someone else supports a candidate?
Am I willing to let the Holy Spirit lead me in making the right decision?

Prayer

Father, we ask You in the name of Jesus to forgive us for anytime that we have voted for a candidate without first consulting You. We ask that You give us wisdom and guidance in our decision-making. Help us to check the voting record of each candidate and see where they stand on the issues that are important to You. Let us not take our vote for granted. Let us voice our opinion and support the issues that are important to You. Lord, let us be an instrument for Your word and continue to inform others about You and Your goodness. Let us pray for candidates that truly represent You so that Your will may be accomplished. I pray for unity among both parties. May they seek You in all their decision-making regardless of the party they are affiliated with. Let our focus be on You and not our own personal agenda. In the Jesus name we pray. Amen.

Biblical References – Moral Checkup

But when he, the Spirit of truth, comes, he will guide you into all truth. He will not speak on his own; he will speak only what he hears, and he will tell you what is yet to come. John 16:13

Wherefore by their fruits ye shall know them. Not every one that saith unto me, Lord, Lord, shall enter into the kingdom of heaven; but he that doeth the will of my Father which is in heaven. Matthew 7:20-21

Commit thy works unto the Lord, and thy thoughts shall be established. Proverbs 16:3

A man's heart deviseth his way: but the Lord directeth his steps. Proverbs 16:9

The fear of the Lord is the beginning of knowledge: but fools despise wisdom and instruction. Proverbs 1:7

Trust in the Lord with all thine heart; and lean not unto thine own understanding. In all thy ways acknowledge him and he shall direct thy paths. Proverbs 3:5,6

Be not wise in thine own eyes: fear the Lord, and depart from evil. Proverbs 3:7

Chapter Two

What Issues
Are Important To God?

"He that hath ears to hear, let him hear" (Matthew 11:15).

There are many issues that are important to me because of my culture. I believe in supporting the poor and needy and I give to organizations whose focus is on the poor. I also believe in justice for all men and women. I believe that African-Americans and all people should be given fair treatment in hiring and promotional opportunities. I believe that while we should abstain from breaking the law, there should be equal justice for all men. I believe that women should be given equal consideration for job promotions. The laws are set up in such a way that when an African-American male commits a crime, they automatically go to jail for most of their lives. They usually cannot afford a high-priced attorney and are just processed through the prison system like mail through the post office. Poor people cannot afford good attorneys and sometimes they do not receive the best counsel. I believe the laws are unbalanced and a good example is the law for drugs for crack versus cocaine. One comes with a higher sentence than the other when they should be equal since both are bad. I believe in unity between all men and that we are all created equal. Again, these are my opinions. Are these opinions justified? This is why we have to go to the Word of God. I can be unbalanced and only support only these issues.

Many of these issues often divides the Democrats and the Republicans. Both sides make a case that their values are based on God's values. As a whole, the Democrats say God cares about the poor and the needy, God does not discriminate and He loves all people. God cares about the common man, healthcare, education, Social Security, etc. If we take care of the poor and needy, God will take care of us. Do not look down on other people. All men are created equal in the eyes of God. The Republican platform is o that we should live morally right according to God's word. They also support the poor and needy. They usually support corporate America. We must be careful that we do not become imbalanced. God is a God to all people who accept Him. Our views should be based on the Word of God. There are many times a person will be vocal about one issue while disregarding another. God's views should be our views as Christians. The Bible is a first and final source and God said He is Alpha and Omega, the beginning and the end. While we may have passionate feelings about an issue, we have to see if that passion aligns with God's passion.

The question again is; what issues are important to God?

According to George May, "the issues that are important to God are justice, mercy, and faithfulness."[1] Matthew 23:23 says:

> ***Woe to you, scribes and Pharisees, hypocrites! For you pay tithe of mint and anise and cumin, and have neglected the weightier matters of the law: justice and mercy and faith. These you ought to have done, without leaving the others undone.***

Jesus said this to the Pharisees because he wanted them to continue paying attention to the weightier matters such as justice, mercy and faith and continue to tithe. He condemned them because they wanted to hold the Gentiles to the law that they were not able to keep themselves. This is very apparent in today's political society. We are ignoring the weightier matters: justice, mercy and faith. There is injustice in the prison system. We are quick to condemn a person instead of showing the mercy of Jesus. We are not faithful to God in our daily walk. As a Christian, there has to be balance. We cannot be too far to the left and too far to the right. The Word of God is balanced. We could find ourselves being against abortion and still treat people unfairly because of their race or gender. We could find ourselves taking care of the poor and needy and ignoring laws that protect women or children. This is not an implication that one party does this versus another, but it is an example of how we can support one cause and neglect "weightier matters".

Jesus said "these you ought to have done, without leaving the others undone". It is not about being left-winged or right-winged. Jesus could reach out to anyone in any situation and He never thought he was so untouchable that He could not minister to someone. He had the power to deliver them out of their situation. He has the power to deliver the homosexuals, murderers, thieves, liars, and drug addicts. He has all power. He left us with that power through the Holy Spirit. Too many times we want to limit God and put Him in box. God is omnipotent (all powerful). God is omniscient (knows all things). God is Omnipresent (everywhere).

While it is easy to choose a party and go down the ballot and vote for everyone down the party line, you have to vote for the person the Holy Spirit leads you to vote for. No party totally represents God. As a Christian, you should totally represent God.

Many issues are important to God and the most talked about issues of today are. Murder, Abortion, Healthcare, Education, Morals, Discrimination, Affirmative Action, Prosperity, War, Peace, Injustice and the list could go on and on.

I would like to take a spiritual look at murder. The reason it is wrong is in direct contrast to God's Word which is the final authority. The Bible specifically says in the Ten commandments that thou shalt not kill. Abortion is also the topic that swayed the voters during the 2004 election. What is abortion? Abortion is killing a child before they are fully developed or born. The Bible says life begins at conception. The law says it is okay kill a baby in the first trimester.

"From a Biblical perspective the book of Jeremiah and the book of Psalms tells us,' More importantly, God reveals to us in His Word that not only does life begin at conception, but He knows who we are even before we were formed (Jeremiah 1:5). King David said this about God's role in our conception:' *'For You formed my inward parts; You covered me in my mother's womb. Your eyes saw my substance, being yet unformed. And in Your book they all were written, The days fashioned for me, When as yet there were none of them"* (Psalm 139:13, 16).

On Bible.com we are given an example of how the law was interpreted in the Word of God. "In **Exodus 21:22** God gives a specific law regarding social order for the Israelites. He stated that if two men were fighting and hit a pregnant woman, thus causing her to give birth prematurely; they must be fined according to any damage done to the baby. The fine must be paid in relation to the amount of damage inflicted upon the child. If God would make a law specifically referring to the rights of the unborn, then surely the unborn must mean something to Him!" [3]

The law allows you to have an abortion up to and including three months. The question that arises is when does life begin. Does life begin when the child is born into the world or does life begins when at conception? Science tells us when life begins. "A new individual human being begins at fertilization, when the sperm and ovum meet to form a single cell. "[4] Also, there are tremendous psychological effects of having an abortion.

"Clinical research provides a growing body of scientific evidence that having an abortion can cause psychological harm to some women. "Women who report negative after-effects from abortion know exactly what their problem is," observed psychologist Wanda Franz, Ph.D., in a March 1989 congressional hearing on the impact of abortion. "They report horrible nightmares of children calling them from trash cans, of body parts, and blood," Franz told the Congressional panel. "When they are reminded of the abortion," Franz testified, "the women re-experienced it with terrible psychological pain ... They feel worthless and victimized because they failed at the most natural of human activities -- the role of being a mother."" Also, "Researchers on the after-effects of abortion have identified a pattern of psychological problems known as Post-Abortion Syndrome (PAS). Women suffering PAS may experience drug and alcohol abuse, personal relationship disorders, sexual dysfunction, repeated abortions, communications difficulties, damaged self-esteem, and even attempt suicide. Post-Abortion Syndrome appears to be a type of pattern of denial which may last for five to ten years before emotional difficulties surface.'[4]

These are examples of the psychological issues that can occur when having an abortion. Since God has given us a sound mind and He is not the author of confusion, then this cannot be of God. If you have had an abortion this chapter is not to condemn you but inform you of what the word of God says. It is also to encourage you to seek God for forgiveness and to move forward in God. Do not condemn yourself.

Are we willing to let the earthly law dictate how we should follow God's law? While we have legislation in place because God allows us to make our own decisions and we have a free will, our will should be to choose the will of God.

Let us look at Shiphrah and Puah in Exodus chapter 1. They were midwives during Pharaoh's day. He commanded all male children to be killed. The ten commandments had not come forth yet. They were trying to save the male child, the Deliverer, Moses. They did not know this yet but they refused to obey the king and his earthly law which was to kill the male child. They knew it would not please God so they did not kill them. They disobeyed Pharaoh and obeyed God. They told Pharaoh that the babies were coming too fast and they could not stop them.

This should be our standard. Whatever it takes to please God, we will please God. You know in your heart when something is not right. So stand up for righteousness! You do not have to know every word or scripture in the Bible, but you have the Holy Spirit who speaks to you and convicts you. Listen to Him and He will guide you.

He also says that some things are an abomination and detestable to him, which means these are things that he despises. Therefore, we could conclude that these are things that we should not do if we want to inherit the kingdom of God.

Proverbs 12:22 says that lying lips are an abomination to God. Galatians 5:20 – 23 says that adultery, fornication, uncleanness, lasciviousness, idolatry, witchcraft, hatred, variance, emulations, wrath, strife, seditions, heresies, envyings, murders, drunkenness, revellings will keep us from inheriting the kingdom of God.

Since we know these things will keep us from inheriting the kingdom of God, we should conclude that these are things that we should not partake of. For clarity, a list of definitions of these abominations are provided so we can understand what they are so we can stay away from them with the help of the Holy Spirit. The Bible says in the book of **Hosea 4:6 that** *"my people are destroyed for lack of knowledge"*. The excuse of not knowing something does not exclude you from being destroyed. God says in His Word that His people, not the people of the world, but His people, the Christians, are destroyed for lack of knowledge.

Sins also keep us separated from God. There are two types of sins. The sins of omission and the sins of commission. The sin of omission is not doing what God has told you to do like neglecting your prayer life or not taking care of the poor and the needy. The sin of commission is committing a sin and violating God's law. An example would be murder or lying. Please know (learn) these and absorb them in your Spirit so you stay as far away from them as you can. Do not be destroyed for lack of knowledge! If you fall short, quickly ask God for forgiveness and turn towards Him.

According to www.crosswalk.com, these things that are an abomination to God:

Lying lips: a person who lies.

Adultery: Voluntary sexual intercourse between a married person and a partner other than the lawful spouse.

Fornication: Voluntary sexual intercourse between an unmarried person.

Uncleanness: in a moral sense: the impurity of lustful, luxurious, profligate living, Morally defiled; unchaste.

Lasciviousness: unbridled lust, excess, licentiousness, lasciviousness, wantonness, outrageousness, shamelessness, insolence 3, Exciting sexual desires; salacious.

Idolatry: the worship of false gods, idolatry.

Witchcraft: sorcery, magical arts, often found in connection with idolatry and fostered by it.

Hatred: the emotion of hate; a feeling of dislike so strong that it demands action.

Variance: contention, strife, wrangling 3, the state or fact of differing or of being in conflict.

Emulations: an envious and contentious rivalry, jealousy.

Wrath: passion, angry, heat, anger forthwith boiling up and soon subsiding again.

Strife: electioneering or intriguing for office, partisanship, fractiousness.

Seditions: dissension, division.

Heresies: a body of men following their own tenets (sect or party). A controversial or unorthodox opinion or doctrine, as in politics, philosophy, or science.

Envying: prompted by envy, A feeling of discontent and resentment aroused by and in conjunction with desire for the possessions or qualities of another.

Murders: slaughter, To kill, To put an end to.

Drunkenness: – intoxications, To stupefy or excite by the action of a chemical substance such as alcohol.

Reveling: a nocturnal and riotous procession of half drunken and frolicsome fellows who after supper parade through the streets with torches and music in honor of Bacchus or some other deity, and sing and play before houses of male and female friends; hence used generally of feasts and drinking parties that are protracted till late at night and indulge in revelry, A boisterous festivity or celebration; merrymaking

These Things Are Detestable

Unjust weights and measures – Deuteronomy 25:13-16, Proverbs 11:1, 20:1,23.

Idolatry – Deuteronomy 7:25, 27:15, 16.

Uncleanness – Leviticus 18:22.

Incest – Leviticus 18: 6-18.

Lying with a woman in her menses – Leviticus 18:18-20.

Adultery – Leviticus 18:20.

Sodomy – Leviticus 18:22 –23.

You must not bring the earnings of a female prostitute or of a male prostitute into the house of the LORD your God to pay any vow, because the LORD your God detests them both.– Deuteronomy 23:18" [5]

Now that we know the definitions of these, we will not suffer because of lack of knowledge. We will stay far away from these because we know they are not pleasing to God. If we have committed any of these sins or are committing these sins, the only way to get in back relationship with God is to repent. To repent means to turn away from your sins and accept Jesus as your personal savior. If you have accepted Jesus as your personal savior and still struggle with these issues, then acknowledge your sin and seek God for deliverance. You are not alone and we all struggle.

There are other issues that God considers important. The Pharisees asked Jesus what is the greatest commandment. When the Pharisees tried to test Jesus and ask Him what is the greatest law. Matthew 22:36-40 gives us Jesus' response.

"Teacher, which is the greatest commandment in the Law?" Jesus replied: "Love the Lord your God with all your heart and with all your soul and with all your mind. This is the first and greatest commandment. And the second is like it: Love your neighbor as yourself. All the Law and Prophets hang on these two commandments". Imagine that. Love is the most important commandment. Husbands are to love their wives as Christ loves the church. We are to love God our Father and Creator. We are to love our brother (black, white, brown, male, female). We are to be sensitive to the poor and the needy and the hungry. We cannot neglect the poor and say we are of God. We are to love our brothers and sisters as Christ love the church. Check your love walk today. See if you are truly loving as Christ loves. See if you are walking in the love of Jesus with all people. Be careful not to make your race, gender, party, nationality more superior than another or even more important than God. Trust God and seek God in your decision-making. Our first allegiance is not to our race, party, or nationality but it is to God.

Jesus also told us *that above all we should love one another as Christ loved the church (John 13:34).* When you have a foundation of love, it will lead you to make the right decisions. When we love someone, we do not kill, we do not backbite, or turn our head when we see someone hungry. We help the poor and the needy. If we would walk in love, then God will guide us in our decision-making. We will not support one group of people and disregard another. We will not support one nation of people and ignore the people in Sudan, Darfur and the Africans countries that are starving. We would relieve them of the debt they owe and give them a new start.

We will not have a law that allows the Cubans to come to America and turn the Haitians around. We will love all people regardless of race, creed or color.

If someone says, "I love God," and hates his brother, he is a liar; for he who does not love his brother whom he has seen, how can he love God whom he has not seen?"
1 John 4:20

The true test is not only what we say but what we do. How can you say you love God and you are a servant of God but you cannot love your brother who needs your help right now?

Hurricane Katrina and the Tsunami

During the Hurricane Katrina disaster of 2005, the covers were pulled back and America saw first hand how the poor, which consisted mainly of African-Americans, were living. They have been living in poverty for years. While America stood in shock and in complete disarray, people were scrambling for their lives, unable to help their loved ones who were trapped in houses. Family members had to choose who to help and who to leave. The dependency on government left the victims helpless. When the Tsunami hit, America was able to mobilize and lend its support to help the victims. The Tsunami caught the world off guard and killed 70,000 people. America was able to setup support systems, provide food and lend help in a time of need, but for some reason when Hurricane Katrina stormed through the gulf coast, America was paralyzed. People were unable to communicate, unable to develop a plan of action, unable to help the hurting and hurting people who were in need. Comments were made that the people are better off now than they were before. There was an insensitivity to the poor. God had positioned the church to step up to the plate and help. The church stood up during this time and took and claimed her rightful place. We are to be the salt of the earth (Matthew 5:13). We are to be light of the world (Matthew 5:14). We need to learn to depend on God. We have been commanded to take care of the poor. "If one of your brethren becomes poor, and falls into poverty among you, then you shall help him, like a stranger or a sojourner, that he may live with you" Leviticus 25:35

Another important issue that is often overlooked is salvation. Everything rests on salvation. John 3:16 (NIV) states it best. It states "For God so loved the world that He gave his only begotten Son, that whoever believes in Him should not perish but have everlasting life". Now that is real love. 2 Corinthians 5:21 (NIV) states "For He made Him who knew no sin [That's Jesus] to be sin for us, that we might become the righteousness of God in Him". God loves the world. That means everyone: white, black, brown, male, female. He even loves homosexuals, lesbians, murderers, and everyone. The sin is an abomination to Him but he loves everyone. Do not let your sin separate you from God. Since he loves everyone, everyone has the opportunity to come into reconciliation with God through Christ Jesus. If you choose to reject this free gift, then you will not inherit the Kingdom of God. Paul said in Romans 10:13 (NIV) *"everyone that calls on the name of the Lord shall be saved".* Romans 10:9-10 (NIV) states *"that if you confess with your mouth, 'Jesus is Lord', and believe in your in your heart that God raised him from the dead, you will be saved. For it is with your heart that you believe and are justified, and it is with your mouth that you confess and are saved".* This is more important than anything else. This is what our lives are all about, salvation and showing the love of Jesus. While we focus on so many other things such as capital punishment, the poor and needy, health, prosperity, healthcare, education and morals, it all still rests on salvation. If we are not saved and we are fighting for all these other things, it will not matter anyway.

Be balanced. Know what is important to God. Be fair. Embrace justice, mercy and faithfulness. Fight the good fight of faith and allow the Holy Spirit to speak to your heart and move forward with His guidance.

Growing Morally Questions
Am I staying away from the things that are detestable and is an abomination to God?
Am I obeying part of God's word and ignoring the weightier matters?
Have I confessed with my mouth and do I believe in my heart that Jesus died on the cross and rose from the dead?
Am I saved?

Prayer

Lord, God we come to You asking You to forgive us for anytime that we obeyed a portion of your word and ignored the other. Let us not have a Pharisee-like spirit and look down on others for their sins when we are still falling short. Forgive us for committing detestable and abominable sins. Lord, if we fall into any of those categories, help us to repent and turn away from my wickedness. We know that we will never be perfect and we thank you for your grace and mercy that covers us. Lord if we do not know You as our personal savior, let us make You Lord over our lives. I confess with my mouth and believe in my heart that Jesus died on the cross and rose from the dead. Thank You Lord that now I am saved. In Jesus name, Amen.

Biblical References – Moral Checkup

Woe to you, scribes and Pharisees, hypocrites! For you pay tithe of mint and anise and cumin, and have neglected the weightier matters of the law: justice and mercy and faith. These you ought to have done, without leaving the others undone. Matthew 23:23

We know that the law is good if one uses it properly. We also know that law is made not for the righteous but for lawbreakers and rebels, the ungodly and sinful, the unholy and irreligious; for those who kill their fathers or mothers, for murderers, for adulterers and perverts, for slave traders and liars and perjurers—and for whatever else is contrary to the sound doctrine that conforms to the glorious gospel of the blessed God, which he entrusted to me. 1 Timothy 1:8-11

The LORD detests lying lips, but he delights in men who are truthful. Proverbs 12:22

The acts of the sinful nature are obvious: sexual immorality, impurity and debauchery; idolatry and witchcraft; hatred, discord, jealousy, fits of rage, selfish ambition, dissensions, factions and envy; drunkenness, orgies, and the like. I warn you, as I did before, that those who live like this will not inherit the kingdom of God. But the fruit of the Spirit is love, joy, peace, patience, kindness, goodness, faithfulness, gentleness and self-control. Against such things there is no law. Galatians 5:19 – 23

For God so loved the world that he gave his one and only Son, that whoever believes in him shall not perish but have eternal life. John 3:16

For He made Him who knew no sin to be sin for us, that we might become the righteousness of God in Him. 2 Corinthians 5:21

That if you confess with your mouth, "Jesus is Lord," and believe in your heart that God raised him from the dead, you will be saved. For it is with your heart that you believe and are justified, and it is with your mouth that you confess and are saved. As the Scripture says, "Anyone who trusts in him will never be put to shame." For there is no difference between Jew and Gentile—the same Lord is Lord of all and richly blesses all who call on him, for, "Everyone who calls on the name of the Lord will be saved." Romans 10:9-13

This is what the LORD Almighty says: `Administer true justice; show mercy and compassion to one another. Do not oppress the widow or the fatherless, the alien or the poor. In your hearts do not think evil of each other. Zechariah 7:9-10

Freya S. Huffman

Chapter Three

What Party Would Jesus Be Affiliated With?

I know this sounds like a silly question because Jesus will not be coming down to earth to become a citizen of the United States. This question was asked because as a Christian, our foundational belief is Jesus is the Son of God and we are to follow His example. Jesus is our guide and our example. We do not have to go far to look at Jesus' example in dealing with groups of people. He took every opportunity to teach, train and change the world around Him. Jesus often dealt with the Pharisees and the Sadducees because these were the political groups in His day. According to Lea and Hudson, the Pharisees were the largest and most influential sect. They kept the law rigidly and believed in the existence of angels and spirits, and expected a resurrection of the body. "The Sadducees were fewer in number than the Pharisees, but they had great political power. Most of the highly priestly families in the New Testament times were Sadducees. The Sadducees followed a literal interpretation of the Law or Torah, accepting only the first five books of the Bible. They rejected the oral tradition the Pharisees accepted. They denied the existence of angels and did not believe in personal immorality. Sadducees were ready to join in support any government that could preserve influence."[1].

When Jesus called the twelve disciples, He commanded them, saying: "Do not go into the way of the Gentiles, and do not enter a city of the Samaritans. But go rather to the lost sheep of the house of Israel. And as you go, preach, saying, 'The kingdom of heaven is at hand.' Heal the sick, cleanse the lepers, raise the dead, cast out demons. Freely you have received, freely give. (**Matthew 10:5-9**). In this scripture, Jesus is showing us that we are to focus on the lost sheep. He is not limiting Himself to one group or another, but His focus is on the lost.

If we look at the party structure today and analyze the parties and what they believe in, we can see which party has characteristics like Jesus. Below is a chart of the issues. You can use this to fill in the blanks to see how each party or candidate stands on these issues.

Issue	Democratic Party Christ Likeness	Republican Party Christ Likeness
Abortion		
Take Care Poor / Needy / Homeless		
Ban Same – Sex Marriage		
Peace		
War		
Affirmative Action		
10 Commandments		
Racism		
Homosexuality		
Education		
Life		
The War on Terrorism		

Commandment	Have you broken any of these?
1. Thou shalt have no other gods before me.	
2.Thou shalt not make unto thee any graven image, or any likeness of any thing that is in heaven above, or that is in the earth beneath, Or that is in the water under the earth:	
3. Thou shalt not take the name of the LORD thy God in vain; for the LORD will not hold him guiltless that taketh his name in vain.	
4. Remember the sabbath day, to keep it holy.	
5. Remember the sabbath day, to keep it holy.	
6. Thou shalt not kill.	
7. Thou shalt not commit adultery.	
8. Thou shalt not steal.	
9. Thou shalt not bear false witness against thy neighbour.	
10. Thou shalt not covet thy neighbour's house, thou shalt not covet thy neighbour's wife, nor his manservant, nor his maidservant, nor his ox, nor his ass, nor any thing that is thy neighbour's.	

The Ten Commandments should be the standard that we live by. The great part about our relationship with Jesus is that although we fall short, because we have accepted Christ as our personal savior we have been reconciled to Christ. When we sin, we should quickly repent and keep moving forward. We could miss heaven if we do not repent. So repent daily because none of us are perfect and all us have fallen short but what brings us back to God is the acceptance of Jesus. We are under God's grace but we should not use this an excuse to sin. Paul said in Romans 6:1, *"Well then, should we keep on sinning so that God can show us more and more of his wonderful grace?"* (New International Version).

We are going to sin. This is inevitable because we were born into sin but when we were born again, Jesus washed away our sins and gave us a way back to our Father, God in Heaven. This is why repentance is so important. Each day we need to wake up with a praise on our hearts. We should then repent for all of our sins, known and unknown which are the sins of commission and omission. Next we should ask God for forgiveness of our sins. We need to forgive those who have hurt us. Lastly we come before Him with our praises and prayers. Using this pattern of prayer ensures that we are in right standing with God on a daily basis. The Bible says to pray without ceasing.

When Jesus was on earth, He taught the disciples and those around Him. His teaching styles as describe by Lea and Hudson:

1. Colorful expressions
2. Authoritative (Mark 1:22, Matthew 5:22, 28, 32, 39, 44)
3. Use of Parables (Luke 7:40-50)
4. Picturesque Speech (Matthew 7:3-5, 23:25-29)
5. Arguments from Scripture (Matthew 22:23-45)
6. Questions and Answers ((Matthew 13:10; Mark 4:10-20)
7. Object Lessons (Matthew 18:1-5; Mark 12:41-44)
8. Frequent Repetitions (Matthew 5:11-12; Luke 6:27-28;
9. Matthew 5:38-42; Luke 6:29-31) [1]

When dealing with people you need all of these teaching characteristics. According to Step by Step Through the new Testament, Jesus' teachings dealt with Moral and Theological subjects, the Kingdom of God, Jews and the Kingdom, the church and the kingdom, and the requirements for entering into heaven. He organized his teachings around His own person. "Jesus never organized His teachings into a system. The value of His teaching stems from his position as God's Son and our Savior." (Step by Step Through the new Testament, Lea, Hudson, Pg. 31)

Jesus healed the sick (Matthew 4:23-25). In the Beatitudes (Matthew 5:1-11), Jesus blesses the people. He talked about where murder begins (Matthew 5:21-26), adultery in the heart (Matthew 5:27-30), Marriage (Matthew 5:31-32), He tells us to love our enemies (Matthew 5:43-48). Jesus did so much and when the Pharisees tried to stump Him with all of these philosophical issues. He handled them with the methods of teaching described above.

Jesus often spoke in parables. An example is, Jesus warned disciples of the leaven of the Pharisees and the Sadducees. They reasoned among themselves, saying 'It is because we have taken no bread'. Verse 11 says:

How is it you do not understand I did not speak to you concerning bread? – but to beware of the leaven of the Pharisees and Sadducees. They understood that He did not tell them to beware of the leaven of bread, but of doctrine of the Pharisees and the Sadducees." Why would Jesus caution the disciples to be cautious of the doctrine of these people who followed God and whose religion was Judaism? My opinion is because He knew their hearts and how they could focus in on one area and exclude others. If we are not careful, we could do the same thing. He warned to watch the leaven. "The leaven could represent yeast. Yeast rises and could represent being puffed up or proud. [2]

One of His most memorable messages to the Scribes and Pharisees was found in Matthew 23.

The scribes and the Pharisees sit in Moses' seat. Therefore whatever they tell you to observe, [1]that observe and do, but do not do according to their works; for they say, and do not do. For they bind heavy burdens, hard to bear, and lay them on men's shoulders; but they themselves will not move them with one of their fingers. But all their works they do to be seen by men. They make their phylacteries broad and enlarge the borders of their garments. They love the best places at feasts, the best seats in the synagogues, greetings in the marketplaces, and to be called by men, 'Rabbi, Rabbi.' But you, do not be called 'Rabbi'; for One is your Teacher, the Christ, and you are all brethren. Do not call anyone on earth your father; for One is your Father, He who is in heaven. And do not be called teachers; for One is your Teacher, the Christ. But he who is greatest among you shall be your servant. And whoever exalts himself will be humbled, and he who humbles himself will be exalted.

Based on this, I do not think Jesus would not have been a Democrat or a Republican. He would have looked at both parties and commended them for the good that they do. He would have also pointed out hypocrisy on both sides. He would have warned us to be cautious and careful and watch the doctrine and stay true to the doctrine of Christ. He said if an angel preaches any other doctrine, reject it.

Jesus also commended and criticized the seven churches in Revelations. When Jesus spoke to the seven churches, He commended them for what they did right. He also showed them the areas He was not pleased with. We are the church. The building is where we worship is also called a church but Christ was talking to the people of God.

In the book of Revelations, Jesus spoke of the seven churches of Asia Minor.

1. ***To the Loveless Church***: He commended them for their works, labor, patience and that they could not bear those that were evil. He still had this against them. They left their first love. Their first love was Christ but they had gotten so busy with their works and their labor that they had neglected their relationship with Christ. This can also be seen when Jesus spoke to Mary and Martha.

2. ***To the Persecuted Church:*** He commended them for their works and how they endured tribulation. He told them to be faithful even until death.

3. ***To the Compromising Church:*** He knew there works and that they held fast to their name and did not deny His faith but He still had this against them. They held the doctrine of Balaam who taught Balak to put a stumbling block before the children of Israel to eat things sacrificed to idols and to commit sexual immorality.

4. ***To the Corrupt Church:*** He commended them for their works, love, service, faith and patience. The thing He had against them is that they allow the woman Jezebel who calls herself a prophetess, to teach and seduce His servants to commit sexual immorality and eat things sacrificed to idols. To know more about the negative effects of the Jezebel spirit and the negative influence, I would urge every Pastor, Leader and Christian to read **Unmasking the Jezebel Spirit** by John Paul Jackson. He went on to be with the Lord in 2015. You will cry out for your church because you will see

why churches are dying out today and why there is so much sickness in the house of God. Satan is busy and he wants to stop the flow of God. He will use anyone who is not prayed up. Members cover your leaders in prayer and when you recognize something that is not of God go into spiritual warfare because God has called us to be watchmen for our presidents, pastors, bosses, leaders, and families.

5. ***To the Dead Church:*** He commended them for their works that they have a name that you are alive, but you are dead. We can be busy doing things in Jesus name, but we can be spiritually dead. We can be revived when we show the love of Christ. When our government is deadlocked and we are unable to pass laws, we are spiritually dead.

6. ***To the Faithful Church:*** He commended them their works and their faithfulness.

7. ***To the Lukewarm church***: He was not pleased because they were neither cold nor hot. Many politicians are lukewarm and God is watching. There are many who are "straddling the fence". There are many who do not want to make a full commitment to God. God is not pleased and said He will spew you out of His mouth. If you are teetering back and forth between the world and God, choose this day whom you will serve. Your choice is Heaven or Hell. Hell is real. In **23 Minutes in Hell**, the Bill Wiese explains vividly how Hell is dark, gloomy and full of torture. The hardest part of being in Hell is knowing that Heaven exists and you cannot even go there because you made the choice to be lukewarm. God loves you so much and He cares all about you. He has set the table for you to receive and all you have to do is

receive the free gift and serve Him with your whole heart. You may have fallen short, but He knows your heart. David did many immoral things but God knew that David had a heart for Him. Choose this day who you will serve. Lukewarm means you do not love God at all in God's eyes. Vote righteously and stand up for what is right.

Jesus came to earth to live as an example for us. He said in his word, "Give to Caesar what is Caesar's and give to God what is God" (Matthew 22:21; Mark 12:17; Luke 20:25). He abided by the laws on earth while he was on earth. He paid taxes. He knew that the taxes would help take care of the earthly government. Our vote should be treated the same way. It was put here for the earthly government.

I believe Jesus would have looked at the candidates and checked their heart to see if they aligned with what was right. If both candidates were wrong, I believe he would have prayed for the right choice and if no candidate met the standard, he would not have voted at all for the candidate.

During the last Presidential election (2004), moral issues played a big part in the voter's decision. The most important issue was abortion. In general the Republicans say that abortion is a sin and the Democrats said it is a woman's choice. This is not inclusive all Democrats and Republicans but this is a general consensus since there are many Christian Democrats who also believe in pro-life. The Democrats also said that Jesus spoke more about taking care of the poor and needy more than killing. I know the perception is that all Democrats are pro-choice but many are against abortion. If you are against abortion, you have to say it.

Every senator, congressman, president or anyone in political office will be held accountable for their choices. We all will be held accountable for our choices. What is our choice? Our choice is our vote! I do not know if Jesus would have been affiliated with any party. I do think He would have voted for what was right according to the will of God if he were a citizen of the United States. We know His citizenship was in Heaven but if He were man only and lived within this society as a man, not the son of God, but as a born again believer, he would have voted according to the word of God or maybe he would not have voted at all. He would have set an example by speaking up for what is right.

When the Pharisees brought the adulterous woman before Jesus after catching her in the act, they wanted Him to persecute her. According to their law, she was to be stoned. Instead Jesus said let him who is without sin cast the first stone. He also said, "where were your accusers?" She said there are none. He told her to go and sin no more. He did not condone her action neither did he condemn her. If the word of God says do not steal but the law says it's okay to steal, you will not be punished. Which law do you follow? This is the same issue that we are dealing with concerning abortion. The word of God says do not kill so we should follow God's law.

God gave us a free will. He gave us the free will to accept Jesus as our Lord and Savior so having an abortion should be a woman's free will, right? While it may be a woman's free will, it still violates the word of God. All of our choices are our own will. The problem comes in when you compare it to the ten commandments, "thou shalt not kill". Having an abortion is in direct violation of God's commandment, which makes it a sin. The death penalty also involves killing. It should also be scrutinized against the Word of God. There are no commandments that say thou shalt feed the poor, although it is required of us.

God will speak to the prophets and tell them what is important and what we must focus on. What we are saying when we make the statement, "it is a woman's right to choose" is that we will not personally have an abortion but we will support another's choice to have an abortion. The Bible says that a man should not be double-minded in his ways. When we make a comment that we are being double-minded. The Lord says in his word that when you are lukewarm, he will cast you out of his sight. The Lord is looking for a people who will stand up for what is right. Yes, you have a right to make the decisions you want however if it does not align with the word of God, it is not right.

The Lord says in his word that we are to be the light of the world. The world should want to be like us. We can minister to the poor and their situation can change but once you have an abortion, the baby can not be brought back to life! See the difference? We must also look at other issues such as feeding the poor, greed, peace, war and morals. We must consider all the issues and not make the moral litmus test abortion only.

We should pray and seek God to see what He is saying at this time and trust Him in our decision-making and not rely on our flesh.

We must follow Jesus' characteristics and His ways. We must allow the Holy Spirit to speak to us when making decisions and we must pray to God and pray that we will be used as a vessel for His work. Jesus charged us all to go and make disciples of men. He told us the greatest commandment is to love one another. You do not kill what you love. You do not neglect what you love. You do discriminate against what you love. We should all embrace the greatest commandment and do as Jesus did, love one another as Christ loves the church.

Growing Morally Questions
Do I support abortion?
Do I support candidates that support abortion?
Have I checked the voting records of my candidate?
Do I know their views on abortion?
Do I support the poor and needy?
Am I morally balanced?
Am I following Jesus' methods?

Prayer

Father, we ask You in the Holy name of Jesus to help us support the issues that are important to You. Forgive us for supporting anything that does not align with Your word. Lord change our hearts if we support issues such as abortion, neglecting the poor and needy, and racism. Lord if we have had an abortion, we ask for Your forgiveness since we now know that killing is a sin. Please lead us to make the right decisions in this area from now on and tell others who may be in error of what Your word says. Help us to check the voting records of the candidates and check their values to see what they stand for. If they do not align with your word Lord God, please lead us to the candidate that does. We know the candidates running for political office will not be perfect, but we know there are those who have a personal relationship with and desire to do your will. We ask you for direction. We ask all of this in Jesus name we pray. Amen.

Biblical References – Moral Checkup

And it seems evil to you to serve the Lord, choose yourselves this day who you will serve ... as for me and my house, we will serve the Lord. Joshua 24:15

And Elijah came to all people, and said, 'How long will you falter between two opinions? If the Lord is God, follow Him; but if Baal, follow him. 1 Kings 18:21

I am the way and the truth and the life. No one comes to the Father except through me. John 14:6

Freya S. Huffman

Chapter Four

Why Vote?

For as the body without the spirit is dead, so faith without works is dead also (James 2:26).

Voting has been a part of this world since the men first cast lots in the Bible. Lots represented votes. Dictionary.com says the definition of voting is "A formal expression of preference for a candidate for office or for a proposed resolution of an issue." Whenever a decision has to be made, people usually depend on the vote to make the final decision. This is usually because discussion alone did not bring the participants into unanimous agreement. Therefore, voting or casting lots is used to make the decisions based on the majority's view. Voting is used in board rooms, interviews, neighborhood covenants, organizations, and even used to pick a captain in a simple game of kickball. Voting implies authority. When you vote it means you have authority to support an idea, a person, an establishment or disagree with an idea, a person or an establishment.

There are two groups of non-voters. One believes their vote does not make a difference and the other feels they should not be involved in politics because of their religious beliefs. First, I will address the non-voters who choose not to vote because they feel that it does not make a difference. The Presidential elections of 200 and 2004 were determined by two states respectively, Florida and Ohio. This is the world that we live in and we have a chance to create the society that we should live in. When we choose not to partake in the voting process we are leaving the world to create a society in which we have no input. If a law is created to make all second graders stay in school for twelve hours and we do not vote on it, then we have lost our right to say anything about it later. When you choose to speak up for what you believe in, it is essentially a vote. You are voicing your opinion on a matter and hopefully that opinion reflects God's values. Your vote is your tool to voice your opinion. When you speak out about issues, you are letting people know your point of view. This is what we do in our daily conversation, we voice our opinion on certain issues. A vote is just an extension of that.

At one time in history African-Americans and women did not have the right to vote and their voice was not heard. They had to live by the laws that only white men created. When they became vocal, laws were changed, and views were taken into consideration. They can now vote for Presidential elections and local elections. Imagine what this world would be like today if minorities and women could not vote? When we choose not to vote, we are leaving our power on the table for others to use.

As Christians, we are not of this world but we live in this world and we have to adapt to the laws that are put in place. Does it make sense to allow a government to put laws in place and we just abide by them with no voice? If we have the opportunity to make the world a better place with our vote, does it make sense to do this? Let us say there is a law that says that kids only go to school up to the third grade and after that they have to educate themselves. Now as parents we would be outraged. If we do not vote and allow this law to take place, then we are responsible for all the children's education stopping at the third grade because we chose not to vote. We have to live in this society and we have the power to influence it according to the values and views that God has instilled in us. The Holy Spirit guides us based on what God has established. Our vote is an extension of our beliefs and our beliefs as Christians should be what the Word of God says. The Holy Spirit will lead us into all truth.

God is calling His people out from the undercover roles they have been playing as Christians. He is calling His sheep from behind the walls of silence and he wants us to share our true Christian beliefs. If we are Christians, then the world needs to know this not just from lip service but through our vote. Many make the comment that I would do something if I could or I sure wish they would change that law. Your ability to set up a Godly government lies in your vote. Many of us are undercover Christians. An undercover person is one who conceals their identity. They do not want anyone to know who they really are. It is a form of deception. They have a secret identity. To keep you from knowing who they really are, they act or behave differently. God says is if you deny Him before men, He will deny you before the Father. Are you an undercover Christian? As Christian people, the world needs to know what we stand for. What do we stand for? Hopefully we stand for the Word of God.

Luke 9:26 tells us "If anyone is **ashamed** of **me** and my words, the Son of Man will be **ashamed** of him when he comes in his glory and in the glory of the Father and of the holy angels." Who are we trying to please, man or God? If the Word of God says that killing is wrong, then when it is time to vote for legally killing babies through abortion or for the death penalty, you should run to the poles and vote an astounding NO! You are not of this world, and this means you belong to God. Not being of this world means that I do not live for Satan but I live for Christ Jesus although I live on earth. God has given us power and it is time to stop letting Satan influence us in our decisions. It is time to stop being an idle Christian with no voice.

Why vote? We have the power to change our world to reflect God's views until He calls us home. Our children have to grow up and we have to live here until the coming of Christ Jesus. We need to set up a government for our children to live in just as Abraham, Isaac, Jacob and Noah did. We have been given the torch to pass on to future generations. What type of fire will be in your torch? Will it be the fire of the Holy Spirit or the fire of Satan and Hell. Someday when we get to heaven, we may ask Jesus why did you let prayer leave school and I believe he will turn around and answer why did you let prayer leave the school? I gave you all power. I gave you all authority but you did not exercise it. God is in control and He has given all power to us through the Holy Spirit. Faith without works is dead **(James 2:20, 26).** God can do anything but if we have been charged to govern this earth, then we choose what type of world do we want to live in. You can decide with your vote!

To the voters, vote your God-given values. Vote righteously! Vote for candidates that reflect God's values. This is where the rubber meets the road. God knows your heart. Speak up about the things that are not of God. Speak out against neglecting the poor. Speak out against corporations mismanaging their employees' retirement. Speak out against abortion. Speak out against the marriage union if it is not of God. Speak out against taking away social security from the elderly. Speak out against child abuse. Speak out against racism. Speak out against prejudice in the workplace. Speak out against neglect. Speak out against domestic violence. God gave you a voice, so use it!

Growing Morally Questions
Am I an undercover Christian?
Do I support Christ's values openly?
Do I vote?
Am I willing to vote for issues that make my world a better place to live?
Am I setting up a government based on God's word for future generations?

Prayer

Father, we praise You in the name of Jesus Christ. We thank You so much for blessing us with freedom. Lord many countries do not share the same freedoms that we have here within the United States. Many have laws that are forced upon them. Lord many are persecuted and jailed for just sharing your word. Thank you Lord that You allowed us to be born into a country that allows us to exercise our freedoms. We ask You in Jesus name to help me understand how important voting is and our place in society. Let our opinion be based on Your Word and let it be shown in our vote. Let our vote be an extension of the values that You have placed in us. Let us not take our vote for granted. Let us use our vote to create an environment that is pleasing to You. Let us use our vote to vote for acts of peace, to help the poor and needy and to create a safe environment for our children to grow up in. We pray this in Jesus holy name. Amen.

Biblical References – Moral Checkup

But without faith it is impossible to please Him, for he who comes to God must believe that He is, and that He is a rewarder of those who diligently seek Him. Hebrews 11:6

But do you want to know, O foolish man, that faith without works is dead? James 2:20

What does it profit, my brethren, if someone says he has faith but does not have works? Can faith save him? If a brother or sister is naked and destitute of daily food, and one of you says to them, "Depart in peace, be warmed

and filled," but you do not give them the things which are needed for the body, what does it profit? James 2:14-16

Chapter Five

Should We Mix Religion And Politics?

For unto us a Child is born, Unto us a Son is given; And the government will be upon His shoulder. And His name will be called Wonderful, Counselor, Mighty God, Everlasting Father, Prince of Peace (Isaiah 9:6).

We have often heard of the phrase the separation of church and state. This phrase originated from Thomas Jefferson who wrote a letter to the Danbury Baptist Association in 1804. (www.wallbuilders.org)

"Jefferson believed that God, not government, was the Author and Source of our rights and that the government, therefore, was to be prevented from interference with those rights. Very simply, the "fence" of the Webster letter and the "wall" of the Danbury letter were *not* to limit religious activities in public; rather they were to limit the power of the government to prohibit or interfere with those expressions." [1]

We have also seen the scripture that says we are not of this world. Many use this as reference that we should not mix religion and politics. We have taken the scripture that we are not of this world to support this statement. When the Pharisees asked Jesus if they should pay taxes, He asked them to look at the coin and tell Him whose picture was on it. They looked and answered, Caesar's picture was on it. He then said give to Caesar what is Caesar's. If we were not of this world, we would have been exempt from taxes. Jesus did not exempt us. Through this example, He showed us that we are to be law-abiding citizens. Therefore, we need to set up laws that reflect Jesus' values. If we set up a law that is contrary to Jesus, then we have put ourselves in a position to disobey God. Although Jesus lived during Caesar's time, He still abided by the laws of the land. He even influenced the time that He was in. As Christians we should model Jesus' example and abide by the laws of land and use our voice to speak up against unjust laws. Jesus spoke on divorce, which is a social issue. He also spoke on taking care of the poor and needy and love.

In an open letter, Christian Leaders Urge 'Biblical Vote',

"71 evangelical Christian leaders signed a letter that pointed out the ethical issues in the election. Concerning Christians speaking out to influence our nation's issues, the leaders stated:

> "As Christian leaders we agree that the primary message of the New Testament is the good news about salvation through faith in Jesus Christ. But the primary message is not the whole message, and another significant part of the New Testament teaches us how people should live... the Bible also teaches us about what kinds of laws governments should have. The laws of a nation have a significant influence on the nation's moral climate, for good or for ill. This is because laws can either restrain evil or encourage it, and because laws also have a teaching function as they inform people about what a government thinks to be right and wrong conduct. Therefore, we urge pastors and Bible study leaders to teach on these crucial ethical issues facing our nation. We urge all Christians that they have a moral obligation to learn about the candidates' positions, to be informed, and to vote. We urge all

Christians to pray that truthful speech and right conduct on both sides would prevail in this election." [2]

In the open letter, examples in the Bible were used to show how Christians spoke out about ethical issues in government.

• Daniel told King Nebuchadnezzar to practice righteousness and show mercy to the oppressed (Daniel 4:27) [2]
• Old Testament prophets spoke to foreign nations (Isaiah 13-23; Ezekiel 25-32; Amos 1-2; Obadiah to Edom; Jonah to Ninevah; Habbakuk 2, Zephaniah 2) [2]
• Paul spoke to the Roman governor Felix "about righteousness and self-control and coming judgment (Acts 24:25) [2]

A more recent example of speaking out against issues that affect the church can be seen when Christian leaders stood against the Hate Crimes Bill. This bill was created to stop hate crimes in America. This sounds like a noble thing. We have been called to love our neighbors as ourselves. The issue with this bill is that the devil is in the details according to www.traditionalvalues.org.

"The Devil's In The Details Of Daschle's Hate Crime Bill
Washington, DC - It has been wisely said that the "Devil's in the details" of contracts and legislative proposals. That certainly applies to Senator Tom Daschle's bill, S. 19, known as the "Protecting Civil Rights for All Americans Act." S. 19, which few Americans even know about or understand, is on a fast track through the U.S. Senate without much debate or publicity. Yet, this bill doesn't contain just one devil in the details; it contains a virtual legion of demons that will drastically change our social and

political landscape for decades to come and seriously undermine our First Amendment rights to freedom of speech and religion."[3]

According to the High Impact Leadership Coalition,

Christian clergymen and people of faith are making a stand today for religious liberty. WE OPPOSE S.1105, the so-called "hate crimes" bill. Similar law at the state level and in other countries have already been used to muzzle the church. Labeling politically incorrect views as "hate" will have a chilling effect on the free speech and religious liberty of our churches and of our members. Let's be clear: Violent crimes should always be punished, no matter the victim – but thoughts and opinions should never be. Laws punishing violent crime already exist in all 50 states. So, what then will define "hate?" Simply, opposition to homosexuality. Such laws will ultimately establish, as a matter of legal principle, that any opposition to homosexual behavior is inherently a form of "hate," a direct threat to every American citizen's freedom of conscience. This legislation is constitutionally suspect, unnecessary, unfair, and ultimately un-American. We are African Americans, though we represent thousands of Christian leaders of all races. We understand more clearly than most the dangers of racially motivated violence. But we also recognize the threat to religious liberty from labeling Biblical teaching as "hate." The Black community needs a free black pulpit. Indeed, ALL Americans need free pulpits. We urge the Senate to avoid putting America on a road toward forfeiting our most basic freedoms – our freedom of speech, freedom of conscience, and the freedom to exercise religion. WHAT CAN <u>YOU</u> DO? We urge all concerned citizens

to call their Senators (202-224-3121) and call the President (202-456-1111) to express concern regarding S.1105. We stand in unison _AGAINST_ S.1105. Let's Keep Home Alive! [4]

We have the right to speak up against laws that contradict God's word as ambassadors of Christ. If we allow Senators and Congressmen to sponsor a bill that shuts the mouths of God's people, then we are allowing the devil to have his way. Christians should not hate those that do not embody the lifestyle that we do. We should stand against immorality but sharing our disagreements and sharing why we believe what we believe. This is not hate. Hate is when one seeks to hurt another person for their beliefs. We have our beliefs because of whom we serve. When we do not pay attention to the news or what is going on in politics, we have given the enemy free reign.

This is admirable of the pastors who stood against this bill. Many Christians are spiritually asleep and we are to be watchmen. A watchman is one who looks out for trouble. In Matthew 26:36-46, we can see how important being a watchman was to Jesus.

Then Jesus came with them to a place called Gethsemane, and said to the disciples, "Sit here while I go and pray over there." And He took with Him Peter and the two sons of Zebedee, and He began to be sorrowful and deeply distressed. Then He said to them, "My soul is exceedingly sorrowful, even to death. Stay here and watch with Me." He went a little farther and fell on His face, and prayed, saying, "O My Father, if it is possible, let this cup pass from Me; nevertheless, not as I will, but as You will." Then He came to the disciples and found them sleeping, and said to Peter, "What! Could you not watch with Me one hour? Watch and pray, lest you enter into temptation. The spirit indeed is willing, but the flesh is weak." Again, a second time, He went away and prayed, saying, "O My Father, if this cup cannot pass away from Me unless I drink it, Your will be done." And He came and found them asleep again, for their eyes were heavy. So He left them, went away again, and prayed the third time, saying the same words. Then He came to His disciples and said to them, "Are you still sleeping and resting? Behold, the hour is at hand, and the Son of Man is being betrayed into the hands of sinners. Rise, let us be going. See, My betrayer is at hand."

They were asleep and like them, many Christians are spiritually asleep. These ministers saw loop holes in this bill that would include punishment for preaching the word of God and calling it a hate crime. Had they not stood against this bill, Satan would have wiggled into our churches as shut down most of what Christians believe. Thank God for these ministers of the gospel who stood up for righteousness and defeated the enemy! They are true watchmen of the gospel of Jesus Christ. This is what Jesus was urging the disciples to do, be watchmen lest they enter into temptation.

The law is important and we should follow it. We also have to prevent ungodly legislation and protect the gospel of Jesus Christ.

Paul tells Timothy in verse 5 of Chapter 1,

The purpose of the commandment is love from a pure heart from a good conscience, and from sincere faith, from which some have strayed, have turned aside to idle talk, desiring to be teachers of the law, understanding neither what they say nor the things they affirm. 9 But we know that the law is good if one uses it lawfully, knowing this: that the law is not made for a righteous person, but for the lawless and insubordinate, for the ungodly and for the sinners, for the unholy and profane, for murderers of fathers and mothers, for manslayers, for fornicators, for sodomites, for kidnappers, for liars, for perjurers, and if there is any other thing that is contrary to sound doctrine, according to the glorious gospel of the blessed God which was committed to my trust.

The book of Jeremiah tells us about the true heart.

The heart is deceitful above all things, And desperately wicked; Who can know it? I, the LORD, search the heart, test the mind, Even to give every man according to his ways, According to the fruit of his doings. Jeremiah 17:9-10

David asked God to create in him a clean heart in the book of Psalms. In **Matters of the Heart**, Juanita Bynum challenges us to receive a new heart. Our old heart cannot love on its own or receive the word of God. She says that many of us need a heart transplant because according to the book of Jeremiah, our current heart is "deceitful above all things and desperately wicked". "Thus you cannot walk in God's ways unless you fear Him as God – escape Him – a fear that submits to Him, totally and completely. Above this, you cannot walk in His ways unless you love Him from the center of your being, your heart" (**Matters of the Heart, pg 10, Bynum**).

The reason I put such emphasis on the heart is because a heart was made to love. The greatest commandment Jesus gave us was to love one another. The reason we have an issue reconciling is because we allow our difference in opinion to become more important than the Word of God. If the Word is our foundation and our focus, this animosity and strife between Christian politicians should not exist. The strife and animosity is not only party against party but also within the parties. Just as there is always a battle between good and evil in the spirit realm, when we allow Satan to use us for his tactics, we will continue to battle against good and evil in the natural realm.

When dealing with the Pharisees, Jesus often checked their heart. Jesus corrected and criticized the Pharisees – they were most the influential sect during that time. Their influence could affect so many people and Jesus often corrected them even though they were right in their own eyes.

Jesus expressed His anger when He cleaned the temple by kicking those out who were buying and selling in the temple. This can be seen in Luke 19:45-47. He said it is written, *"My house is a house of prayer, but you have made it a den of thieves."* Rev. Otis Moss III elaborated on this in his "Disturbing the Peace" message. He spoke of peace keepers versus peace makers and how many are flocking to the church to gain their votes. It is now a marketing strategy to win the elections. Just as Jesus expressed His anger in conducting business in the temple, we must be careful to guard our temples, which are our churches today. Our votes are not for sale and we have to be discerning enough to know who is of God and who is not. If someone is struggling to quote a scripture this is an indication that they are not studying the scripture. They are only learning a scripture for election purposes. Be careful of wolves in sheep's clothing.

Our political parties today are very influential. We, the Christendom, have to influence the society in which we live just as Jesus did. We have the ability to share the gospel of Jesus Christ within in our society. God has His people in the political government. Will you use your voice for God or Satan? The government is upon Jesus' shoulders. We, the ambassadors of

Jesus Christ, should seek the Holy Spirit and allow Him to speak to us on what we should be speaking up for or praying about. While we are not of this world, we can still influence the world with the gospel of Jesus Christ.

Become a world changer and use your vote to shut down laws that come against the word of God. Use your voice to pray against Satan's tactics to destroy God's word. Work together and pray to expose the enemy who is enmity against the word of God. Stand up! Be counted and be heard!

Growing Morally Questions
Will I use my voice in government?
Will I use my voice to support God's values?
Will I influence my culture with my voice?
Will I pray for my government?
Will I speak up for injustice?

Prayer

Father, You said in Your word that the government is upon Your shoulders. Lord, use us to shape this culture. Use us to speak up for injustice. Use us to shape the government and give scriptural insight to our leaders. Use us to pray and fast for our government and our country. We come against every law that would oppose your word. Give us the boldness and love to stand for righteousness. Teach us to be watchmen of the word and increase our spiritual discernment. We want to be doers of Your will so that You might be exalted in Jesus name. Amen.

Biblical References – Moral Checkup

Of the increase of His government and peace There will be no end, Upon the throne of David and over His kingdom, To order it and establish it with judgment and justice From that time forward, even forever. The zeal of the Lord of hosts will perform this. Isaiah 9:7

Therefore submit yourselves to every ordinance of man for the Lord's sake, whether to the king as supreme. 1 Peter 2:13

Chapter Six

Can My Vote Make A Difference?

*"Moreover **you shall select from all the people able men,
such as fear God, men of truth, hating covetousness;
and place such over them to be rulers of thousands,
rulers of hundreds, rulers of fifties, and rulers of tens"**
(Exodus 18:21).*

If you want to know if your vote will cause a change, we do not
have to far to look. Great examples are the Presidential elections of
2000 and 2004. Florida and Ohio were the deciding states. If people
had abstained from voting and they have the right to do that, the
election results would have been totally different. There have been
many laws that have been created or destroyed because of a vote.
The Voting Rights Act was established by voting. D.U.I. (Driving
Under the Influence) was creating by voting. Voting created the
Amber Alert system which notifies the public that a child has gone
missing. Voting created a law that set the speed limits. Voting
abolished slavery. Voting gave women the right to vote. Voting
made President's Day, Memorial Day, Martin Luther King, Jr.,
Labor Day, Thanksgiving and Christmas official holidays. Voting
legalized abortion. Voting made little Lisa class President. Voting
made little Billy captain of the baseball team. Voting placed Helen
Blocker-Adams, the first black woman to run for mayor in Augusta,
Georgia in third place in the Mayoral election. Voting elected
Barack Obama as the first African-American President.

Can your vote cause a change? Yes, it can! God gave us this world to be stewards over it. We should not live in it and not have a voice. We should not sit idly by and allow the law of the land to dictate how we should live, what we should watch or what we should listen to. I often hear people say we are in this world but not of this world and this is used as a justification not to vote. We are not of the sins of this world but we are still a part of this world. The laws govern how we live and Christians still have to abide by the law. We do have a right to use our vote to change the law but we must live by the law.

A vote is a seed for the future. Just as a farmer sows watermelon seeds and expects a watermelon harvest in a few months, we should sow seeds with our vote. We should "sow" our votes to stop abortion. We should "sow" our votes to ban racism. We should "sow" our votes to place people of God in office. Voting for morality in 2004 caused us to bring God back to the forefront. We need to rely on the Holy Spirit for wisdom and guidance because many are tailoring their speeches to include God. Christians have to pray for guidance in the election. We have to see how God is moving and the direction He is taking. We have to be accountable for our decisions and the government we set up. If we sow the right seeds now, we will reap the harvest that we desire the next four years. We have an obligation to get to know the candidates and their platform. We must not be deceived by their words only, but their actions. We also have to pay attention what they aren't saying.

CNN had a forum on faith and politics. This was an opportunity to see the candidate's views on God. Many of the Democratic candidates expressed their position about that their Lord and Savior Jesus Christ. This is the first time that America has seen them express this in an open platform. They know that this Presidential election will be about morals. We have to pray and allow the Holy Spirit to guide us into all truth.

We are to seek God in all of our decision-making and a vote is a decision. You decide to support and disapprove of a decision that someone has set before you.

When Christians sit by and allow others to make decisions that affect our lives, we have lost the opportunity to provide God's input into the political process. We allow the politicians to remove prayer from schools and remove the ten commandments from federal offices. When we do this we are giving Satan free access to our children and our lives with no resistance. He has simply come in and sat right in the middle of the classrooms and his deceiving spirit is causing normal suburban children to gun down their whole school. When you stay out of the political process, you are allowing unfair laws to be in place that are harsher for blacks than whites. When you stay out of the political process you allow teens to be tried as adults, pornography to become legal, and even loop holes to appear in the law. When you stay out of the political process you allow politicians to make decisions that say it is okay for Cubans to come to America but if a Haitian comes, they have to be sent back. We are responsible for putting people in office that reflect Christ's values. Abortion is not the only litmus test. This is but one of the issues that we should look at when we are choosing a candidate. We should also look at the issues that Jesus thought where important: justice, mercy and peace.

Growing Morally Questions
Will I seek God in my decision-making?
Will I talk to my State Representatives about views that are important to me?
Will I vote righteously?

Prayer

Father, give us wisdom in our vote. Show us whom to vote for? Lord You said out of the abundance of the heart the mouth speaks. Give us discernment to hear the heart of man. Give us wisdom in our decision-making and let us listen to the Holy Spirit's leading. Open up our hearts and use us to influence governments and lead the unsaved to Christ in Jesus name.

Biblical References – Moral Checkup

When *the righteous are in authority, the people rejoice; but when a wicked man rules, the people groan. Proverbs 29:2*

And *Jesus came and spoke to them, saying, "All authority has been given to Me in heaven and on earth. Go therefore and make disciples of all the nations… teaching them to observe all things that I have commanded you. Matthew 28:18-20*

Let *every soul be subject to the governing authorities. For there is no authority except from God, and the authorities that exist are appointed by God. Therefore whoever resists the authority resists the ordinance of God, and those who resist will bring judgment on themselves. For rulers are not a terror to good works, but to evil. Do you want to be unafraid of authority? Do what is good, and you will have praise from the same. For he is God's minister to you for good. But if you do evil, be afraid; for he does not bear the sword in vain; for he is God's minister, an avenger to execute wrath on him who practices evil. Romans 13:1-4*

Scriptural Sequence Take from Christian Votes [1]

Chapter Seven

How Do I Know If I Am Voting For The Right Person?

"Yet they will by no means follow a stranger, but will flee from him, for they do not know the voice of strangers" (John 10:5).

In John 10:4 and John 10:27, Jesus says my sheep know my voice and a stranger they will not follow. Christian politicians who vote according to God's will are his sheep; they know his voice. If you are voting your way and your way does not align with the word of God, then you are voting against Him. Are you really his sheep? Since his sheep know his voice, they will know who they should vote for. Sheep have to be guided. You will not follow (or vote for) a stranger as the scripture suggests. How do you get to know his voice? First, you go to the word of God, the Bible. You read and meditate on the Word and know the word for yourself. You do not rely on what others say but you find out what the Bible says. Next "you" pray and "you" seek God for wisdom in your decision-making. There are two parts to voting: natural and spiritual. In the natural, we have an obligation to check out the candidate's background and voting record. Do not take their word for it when they are making their speeches, but go to the library, search the Internet, read the newspapers and check their voting record if one exists. Find out what their views are on God's issues. We discussed those issues in Chapter 2. If their views are contrary to God's, then you need to re-think your vote. Remember your vote is your seed and if you vote for someone who is not seeking God or voting God's way then you are putting people in office who will not vote morally in the future. Many of the people we vote for are put in office for two, four and some even six years. Therefore, if you know they do not share God's values, why put them in office? Party affiliation alone does not make you more of a Christian than someone else. Living a life before Christ and obeying His laws are what makes you a Christian.

Concerning the spiritual side of voting, it has to be partnered with prayer. Voting for a person or issue does not guarantee that a bill will pass. It will set us in the right direction. Praying and seeking God can reach where a vote alone cannot. You are expressing your faith with your vote.

Here is a list to see if you are voting on the right person. I call it a moral litmus test.

- ❑ Does the candidate believe in the Lord Jesus Christ as his personal savior? (Salvation)
- ❑ Does the candidate believe in the Ten Commandments? (Faithfulness)
- ❑ Does the candidate believe in equal treatment of all people? (Justice)
- ❑ Does the candidate believe in supporting the poor and needy? (Mercy)
- ❑ Does the candidate support prayer in schools? (Acknowledging God)
- ❑ Does the candidate love all people? (Love)

While this is not all-inclusive, it does give you a starting point and a guide to voting for the best moral candidate. What if both candidates seem morally right? This is when you have to pray and seek God and trust the Holy Spirit to lead you in making the right decision. The President determines who the next Supreme Court Justices would be. The Supreme Court Justices would determine some of the most important laws which would set the direction of the country for the next 20 or so years. Your vote cannot be cast without a thought; it is a seed that should be prayed over.

When 9/11 hit us and changed our world as we knew it, it was President Bush who called together all the ministers to pray. President George W. Bush had the courage to stand in the face of fear and call together men of God to pray for the direction of the nation. God's will has to be accomplished and He will use who He has to use to do it. If you are not willing to bow down to God, he cannot use you and will choose someone else to do his will. The Lord chose Saul to be King but he turned evil so he used David instead. It took David some years to come into his destiny because he had to fight off Saul and David became King. God told the prophet Samuel to go to (David's father) and choose him. David's father wanted to present some of the older and stronger sons but the prophet had to be faithful to God and ask for the other son, David. David's heart attracted God. God could use him because he would hear from God.

We get caught up in who we want to be in a certain position and we miss what God is saying. This also happens in the church. There are people that God is calling out but the Pastor has His mind on who he wants to use and misses the opportunity to hear from God. I believe there are flaws in both parties. All of us have sinned and have fallen short of the glory of God, but it is the one who is willing to be used by God that God will use. The Bible says that David had a heart after God. David had to kill some smaller giants before he got Goliath. He slew the Lion and the Bear so when he got to Goliath his faith was built up. David was the youngest of all the boys but he loved and trusted in God. God gave him the wisdom and strength to fight Goliath and he defeated him. David defeated him by hitting him in the head with the sling shot. The head represents authority. When you kill the head everything else has to die.

2 Samuel 20 says:

And David said to Abishai, Now Sheba the son of Bichri will do us more harm than Absalom. Take your lord's servants and pursue him, lest he find for himself fortified cities, and escape us.

David said that Sheba would harm them more than Absalom. While God used David mightily, David was not without fault. David had a heart after God but he dealt with lust and other issues. He even killed the husband of the woman that he had an affair with. God still used him after he repented and he was Godly sorry.

There will be other giants that we do not know about but the government does. By killing the little giants, we will be prepared for the bigger giants. I have had to repent and ask God to forgive me for allowing my views to take precedence of what he was saying. He will work out those issues that were important to me. He did it before. He raised up a Martin Luther King, Jr. to fight for civil rights. His one voice gave people the courage from all walks of life to stand up for what was right. President George W. Bush stood up for morality and that is why God could use him. We must still pray for that he will have wise council. Psalm 1:1 tells us not walk in the council of the ungodly. Members of his inner circle resigned because of questionable practices and not being totally honest.

Professing Christ alone is not enough but you must put your faith in action. We have to be sensitive to the Spirit of God in this hour to see what he is saying to us. God will use whom He wants to accomplish His will.

I would like to challenge every candidate, whether Democrat or Republican to stand up for what is right, God's views. Do not stand up as a Republican or a Democrat but as a Christian. If the candidate's views seem to align more with God's issues, then vote for that person not the party. God is challenging us to stand up for what is right, not our favorite person. We may be guilty of doing what I have done in the past, putting my own personal views before God's views. God is looking for some "Davids" to stand up in the face of Satan and say I will use my vote as a seed and choose the one who serves God openly.

In 2004, Democratic presidential candidate Howard Dean told a Tallahassee audience that southerners have to quit basing their votes on "race, guns, God and gays."

In my opinion, this is why Howard Dean went from being the number one Democratic candidate to the bottom of the polls. When you say things such as stop basing the vote on God, that's an abomination to God. It's in direct violation to God's word when he tells us to include Him in all decision-making. We have to think before we speak. If he really meant that then he was not the candidate that God wanted. Should we have voted for him because he was a Democrat? He went from first place to the bottom. Kerry then arose as the Democratic leader. He was a strong leader also, but it still came down to who was willing to stand up for God completely, including mercy, justice and faithfulness.

Our decision-making is vital to our destiny, our blessings and curses. In 1 Kings 22, the King of Israel wanted to go back and take Ramoth Giliead. He asked Jehosophat if he would go fight with him. Jehoshaphat could have said, yes I'll go or no I will not. Instead this was Jehosophat's response, "I am as you are, my people as your people, my horses as your horses." Jehoshaphat also said to the king of Israel, "First seek the counsel of the LORD." The king sent for his 400 prophets and they told him to go and take Ramoth Gilead but he had not sought the council of God. Jehosophat's response was Is there not a prophet of the LORD here whom we can inquire of?" While they were prophets, Jehosophat was looking for a prophet of the Lord. All the other prophets were saying, go attack Ramoth Gilead because the Lord will deliver it to the King's hand. They found a prophet of God, Micaiah. Micaiah did not want to tell them the truth at first and then he prophesied only what God gave him. He did not say what the King wanted him to say nor did he conform to what all the other prophets were saying. He spoke the truth that they would be killed. Although the King disguised himself, he was still killed according to the God's prophet. If the King had listened to God's council, he would have spared his own life. A decision can be life-threatening. Since Jehosophat was obedient, he eventually became king.

It is important to include Christ in your decision-making. Pray for the President regardless of what political party is in office. If the President is a Democrat, Republican or an Independent and they are a Christian, I only hope that we will still show the same type of support because of the office that is represented. Seek Christ as Jehosophat encouraged the King to do. The Holy Spirit will guide you into all truth!

Growing Morally Questions
Have I prayed for the candidates before I made my decision?
Have you performed the moral litmus test on each candidate?
Am I willing to let God lead me in my decision-making?

Prayer

Father, I ask you in the name of Jesus to forgive us for not obeying you when you spoke to us about the candidate we should vote for. Forgive us for putting our personal agenda before your agenda. Lord God, help us to vote your way when we go to the ballot box. Do not allow us to vote along Republican or Democrat party lines, but guide us to vote righteously. Help us to use our vote as a seed that you will allow us to reap a harvest that will help us to live in a morally right government. Have your way in our lives, our thoughts and our actions. We give you the honor, we sit at your feet and we exalt you in Jesus name we pray. Amen.

Biblical References – Moral Checkup

Blessed is the man who walks not in the counsel of the ungodly, nor stands in the path of sinners, nor sits in the seat of the scornful; But his delight is in the law of the LORD, and in His law he meditates day and night. Psalm 1:1-2

Jehoshaphat also said to the king of Israel, First seek the counsel of the LORD. 1 Kings 22:5

Freya S. Huffman

Chapter Eight

Does Voting For A Particular Party Make Me Immoral?

"Romans 3:23 - For all have sinned, and come short of the glory of God" (Romans 3:23).

This question was asked because the Democratic Party has been accused of a party that focuses on social issues and not moral issues. Morals were the deciding factor in the 2004 Presidential election. According to www.dictionary.com, immorality is contrary to established moral principles and morality is the quality of being in accord with standards of right or good conduct. Who makes morals? The Bible is a good source to learn good conduct, thus morality. Democrats are labeled liberals. They also carry the label left-wing. The original term left wing versus right wing originated "from the British House of Commons, where the Popular (Liberal) parties have traditionally sat to the left of the speaker. This term is now used to characterize the Democrats as being left and being wrong while the Republicans are right, morally right. Was the Democratic party established on moral principles? According to the www.democrat.com, the ideas of the Democratic party are:

Prosperity - sustaining and strengthening the economic growth that brought opportunities to so many Americans in the 1990s;

Progress - paying attention to the aspects of our lives that cannot be measured in economic terms but which have a deep impact on our everyday existence; and

Peace - more than just the absence of war it means protecting America's security wherever it is endangered and promoting democratic values around the world."

These are characteristics of Christ and we need to make sure the foundation is Christ. If we are of Christ, we need to say we are of Christ. Division comes when Christ is not our foundation. Before we build anything, there needs to be a strong foundation. Jesus said to Peter "On this rock I will build My church, and the gates of Hades shall not prevail against it" (Matthew 16:18). When a foundation is built on Christ, nothing can prevail against it, not even Satan.

I know many Democrats who are Christians and they have accepted Christ as their personal savior. They are preachers, teachers, lawyers, doctors, and nurses. They love the Lord and serve the Lord but they are professed Democrats. They live right and they do the things that God has called them to do. This picture painted of the Democratic Party because traditionally, Democrats accept all people from all backgrounds and all races. Because of the acceptance of all, this also mean that many ideals and beliefs will also be accepted. We must be careful not to allow these ideals to overshadow Christ's values. If anyone is a Christian Democrat, you are to influence those around you with the Word of God.

In the eyes of the liberal democrats on Liberals for Christ, an organization who comprises of Democrats who serve Christ, the synonyms they found for the word liberal are: tolerant, generous, enlightened, broadminded, lavish and charitable. They see the Conservative as stingy, miserly, regressive, narrow-minded, reactionary, bigoted, prejudiced and biased. These synonyms were retrieved from Roget's Thesaurus. Also in their view, a comparison of the party views is listed below:

"Liberals" on the Left	"Conservatives" on the Right :
Belief in supporting the United Nations & a World Court	Distrust of United Nations & a World Court
Promotion of Unions and Collective Bargaining	Promotion of dog- eat-dog Individualism & "Freedom to Work"
Union of States { National interests } (opposition to slavery)	Dissolution of States { State interests } (defense of slavery

Every human being is entitled to many basic human rights just because they have been born into the human family.	We are born with nothing but the hair on our heads and no right to anything unless and until we or our parents can earn it for us.
Inclusive of All (i.e. those not of the dominant or majority race, religion, class, gender, age, immigration status, sexual orientation, etc.)	Inclusive only of those of one's own class, group, neighborhood, religion, country, etc.,
The instinct of Liberals is to defend the right of their opponents to differ.	The instinct of Conservatives is to suppress dissent .
Elevate the poor	Exploit the poor
promotion of higher minimum wage and even "a Livable Wage"	keep wages as "minimum" as possible (Slave Wages - or free labor was the best !)

promotion of Health Care for all who <u>need</u> it : (Universal Public plan).	Health Care Insurance <u>only</u> for those who can pay for it. (for--Profit Private plans).

Both sides view themselves as champions fighting for liberty, freedom and justice, but they have very different ideas as to whom to protect from whom :

Liberals think that what causes many people to be poor is injustice in the principal transactions of life, i.e. unfair wages for the labor they provide, unfair prices for the goods and services they have to purchase, unfair policies regarding health care, law enforcement, working conditions, discrimination, etc.,	Conservatives think that "successful people" become prosperous by working hard and they need to be defended from the injustice of politicians stealing from the rich to support the lazy.
Promotion of Progressive Taxation of Income (to finance public services).	Opposition to most forms of taxation (and to public services).

as much Equality as possible (e.g. support for taxation of huge estates)	Unlimited Inequality (opposition to taxation of huge estates)
Affirmative Action on behalf of minorities	Negative Inaction benefiting the majority
Freedom for ALL : (requiring restraint of the rich and powerful)	Freedom for the Rich and Powerful : (with as much "deregulation" as possible)

Interested in strong Criminal Prosecution of the crimes

of <u>big</u> people	of <u>little</u> people

Favor strong Religious condemnation of

sins affecting the Public : like greed, political corruption, injustice against whole groups, business malpractice, etc.	Individual or Private sins: like (see website), birth control, abortion, petty theft, etc.
Tend to favor the Gospels of Jesus of Nazareth.	Tend to favor the Epistles of Paul, the "Old Testament" & the Book of Revelation.
Oppose the proliferation of guns, because they end up so often killing innocent people.	Embrace guns, because they enable even weak people the ability to threaten and overpower large numbers of other people.
War is a Last Resort	War is their First Thought

O K with paying taxes, if money is used to care for the needs of others, i.e. the young, old, sick, handicapped, minorities, etc., etc.	O K with paying taxes, if money is used for their own security, i.e. law-enforcement, prisons, and national "defense".
Creativity & New ideas: Liberals respect the ability of all men to think for themselves and welcome and respect new and different insights and discoveries by thinkers in every field. Reason is supreme.	Tradition & Orthodoxy : Conservatives are insecure in their own ability to find the truth and need to have "orthodox" doctrine handed down to them from supernatural authorities. Faith is supreme.

This does not mean all Democrats think this way. It does give a picture of how a party sees themselves and the way they see the other side. On both sides of the columns, there are immoral views. This is why it is so important to use the Word of God as our mirror. When we view each other, we tend to focus on the issues that are important to us. When use the Word of God as our guide, we get a better idea of what Jesus believed.

If we are of Christ, we need to speak up for issues that reflect Christ. "What would Jesus do?" was a popular phrase for a few years. This was the test many used to ensure their actions were equivalent to what Jesus would do in a situation. To expand on this a little more, we should take a look at some issues and see "what Jesus would do?" Would Jesus condone abortion? This is not pleasing to God. God tells us that we shall not kill. Would Jesus take down the Ten Commandments from the courtroom? If this is the law we live by as Christians, I really do not think God will want us to take our law down.

Would Jesus heal the sick? Would Jesus meet the needs of the poor? Would Jesus minister to Homosexuals and Lesbians? Yes, He would; He loves all people. Would Jesus support justice, mercy and peace? There are many questions that we can ask, but we have to seek God in all our questions and all of our decision-making. We do not know everything but the Holy Spirit will guide us into all truth.

Being a Republican or Democrat does not make you moral or immoral. If you are a Christian, research the word of God to see what is being said on a topic. Do not conform to this world but become transformers of this world based on the Word of God!

Growing Morally Questions
Am I willing to stand up for Christ's values?
Will I allow the Holy Spirit guide me into all truth?
Do I allow the Holy Spirit to shape my views and values?
Am I willing to be a voice for Christ in my party?

Prayer

Father, we come to You asking You to help us to live a life that is pleasing to You no matter what our party affiliation may be. Help us to seek You daily and be led by the Holy Spirit daily. If there are any hidden sins, please deal with our hearts so that we may get it right with You. Let us humble ourselves before You and not look down on our brother when they fall. Let us encourage them and pray that they will have a heart of repentance and not downgrade them. Let any leader, public official or anyone of influence check their heart and their lifestyle and make the proper changes today. Let them apologize to those they have hurt including the nation if necessary. For we know that when we humble ourselves before You, You will exalt us. We know we all fall short of your glory so help us to build a circle of Godly people that bear witness with You. Help us to be accountable to the word of God and to each other and walk upright before You. We know we cannot make it in this world alone and the Devil is busy everyday. His job is to kill, steal and destroy. Let us not fall into his trap but we should always watch and pray as Christ commanded us. We continue to seek You in our daily decisions and we pray that we make the moral choices that align with your word regardless of our party affiliation. All these things we ask in Jesus name we pray.

Biblical References – Moral Checkup

The integrity of the upright will guide them, but the perversity of the unfaithful will destroy them. Proverbs 11:3

For the administration of this service not only supplies the needs of the saints, but also is abounding through many thanksgivings to God, while, through the proof of this ministry, they glorify God for the obedience of your confession to the gospel of Christ, and for your liberal sharing with them and all men, and by their prayer for you, who long for you because of the exceeding grace of God in you. 2 Corinthians 9:12-14

But seek first his kingdom and his righteousness, and all these things will be given to you as well. Matthew 6:33

Freya S. Huffman

Chapter Nine

If I Am A Christian Should I Only Vote For A Specific Party?

"Beloved, do not believe every spirit, but test the spirits to see whether they are from God, because many false prophets have gone out into the world" (1 John 1:4).

The Republican Party's platform is a seventy two page document that discusses the issues Republicans support. In searching for the word God, it was found three times. It was mentioned in the context of God blessing Ronald Regan, Faith-based leaders created in the image of God, and not removing God from the Pledge of Allegiance. These are all noble mentions of God. The Republicans are often labeled Conservative or Right-Wing. The definition of conservative is favoring traditional views and values; tending to oppose change; moderate. [1] The term Right-Wing originated from the British House of Commons, where the party has traditionally sat to the right of the speaker. While a label can paint a good picture, the label Republican or Right-Wing alone does not make you right. What makes you right is righteousness in God's eyes. You must believe that Jesus is the son of God and he came to the earth as a sacrifice that we might live.

We must be careful not to adopt a Pharisee spirit. The Pharisees were more concerned with the religious duties instead of embracing Christ. Not all Republicans share "Republican views" nor do all Democrats embrace all "Democratic views". There is not a Christian party, although I propose we start one. There may be people within the party who are Christians but as a whole this party is non-existent. This is proven because many people of political parties do not embrace the party's value system. If we are not careful we can view the party's platform and use this as a foundation to vote along a party line. The people make up the party and it is the people's fruit that we have to check.

Here are some questions to use as a check points. *Do you love unconditionally? Do you take care of the poor and needy? Are you against abortion? Do you say you love all people, but you cannot bear people of another race? Are you running your companies based on God's principles and not working people so much that they do not have time to spend with their families?*

The Democrats see the Republicans as greedy. The Republicans see the Democrats as people who want hand-outs. They have painted this picture because of the Enron and WorldCom examples. These companies went bankrupt when they overstated their earnings and caused the company to fall and tumble along with all the employees' stocks and pensions. Also many look at Republicans as people who favor the rich and neglect the poor. Programs such as Social Security, Welfare, Medicare and National Endowment for the Arts make the top ten list of worst government programs according Human Events nline.[2]

What would Jesus do? Would Jesus put people in jail indefinitely? Would Jesus condone the death penalty? Would Jesus take Social Security away? Would he take away help to get a new home? I do not think He would since He said there will always be poor (Deuteronomy 15:11) and we should take care of the widows (James 1:27) and the elderly. Would Jesus neglect the homeless? No I believe He has commanded us to take care of them. Would Jesus support greed? No, Jesus would tell us that we should all have. If one has more than another then he should help the one who has less.

There should always be balance and the abundance is for those who lack. If we look at the years of famine in Joseph's day, God used Joseph to save his own family because he had an abundance stored up. Joseph faced prison and was thrown away by his family, yet he stood up for morality.

Continue to stand for morality. Continue to pursue goals and dreams but always seek God first. Reach back and help someone else. Apply justice, mercy and peace just as Jesus said these were important matters of the law.

These are things we must consider as Christians. God cares about your heart. First check the candidate's heart by listening to their words and then look at their fruit. Do not be deceived by the party as a whole. Go a step further and check the candidate's fruit.

Prayer

Father, we come to you in the name of Jesus asking you to forgive us for anytime that we have looked down on others or have kept others out of certain positions because of their color or gender. We ask for your guidance in our daily walk and our decision-making. We pray that we would all learn to love one another and be compassionate to those who are different from us. Help us to have the same values in church and in the boardroom. Let us not put our companies in danger by doing things that could hurt other employees. Give us wisdom in all that we do in Jesus name. Amen.

Biblical References – Moral Checkup

He that is faithful in that which is least is faithful also in much: and he that is unjust in the least is unjust also in much. Luke 16:10

A false balance is abomination to the LORD: but a just weight is his delight. Proverbs 11:1

Take us the foxes, the little foxes, that spoil the vines: for our vines have tender grapes. Song of Solomon 2:15

Chapter Ten

Why Do Christian Democrats And Republicans Disagree?

For by one Spirit we were all baptized into one body—whether Jews or Greeks, whether slaves or free—and have all been made to drink into one Spirit. For in fact the body is not one member but many. 1 Corinthians 12:13-14

All who are saved, those who have professed Christ as their personal savior, have the same Spirit of God. Although we may be white, black, Jew, Greek, Gentile, Republican or Democrat, if we are saved, we have the same Spirit. We are children of God. We are servants of Christ. There are disagreements about how to raise children, death penalty, and when life begins. We even have disagreements amongst husbands and wives and siblings. While we will never agree on everything there are some fundamental truths that we must agree on as Christians. We must believe the Bible is true, unadulterated word of God. We must believe that Jesus is the Son of God and died on the cross for our sins. We must follow Jesus' example of love, justice, mercy and peace. We must believe that the Ten Commandments are from God and God left them for us as a guide. Then after we set a firm foundation on the Word of God, issues that arise that do not have an easy answer, should be prayed about. We should allow the Holy Spirit to guide us. Also, discussing the subject with people who are spiritually wiser than you is also something we should consider. When we go to God in prayer, we should seek His wisdom and guidance in our decision-making. 1

Corinthians 1:25 tells us "that God's foolishness is even wiser than men, and the weakness of God is stronger than men." This is why we should "not to lean on our own understanding but in all our ways acknowledge Him and He will direct our paths". Many are directing their paths and depending on their flesh to make their decisions. We are not going to God in prayer before we make our decisions or cast our vote.

Take a look at the two-party system, the visual that comes to mind are two groups of people fighting against one another. Each group has its own set of views and principles that they stand on.

History of the party system

The Democratic Party was established under Thomas Jefferson in the 1790s to resist the policies of the George Washington Administration. The party was originally called the Republican party and later became the Democratic-Republican party. In 1830s the Democratic party, *"It was willing to use national power in foreign affairs when American interests were threatened, but in economic and social policy it stressed the responsibility of government to act cautiously, if at all. Democrats argued that the national government should do nothing the states could do for themselves, and the states nothing that localities could do."[1]*

The parties support included southern plantation owners and immigrant workers in northern cities. They did not like the government intervening in their lives. The Whig party believed "in using governmental power to promote, regulate, correct, and reform". The true division of the Democratic Party came during the North-South conflict concerning slavery. The Democrats wanted to keep slavery and the northerners did not. Many northern Democrats joined the Republican Party. Democrats did not want to increase the tariffs and taxes to finance the Civil War.

"Under the Democratic leadership, the government expanded its role in social welfare and economic regulation. Given the economic situation, this proved to be attractive. Traditional Democrats surged to the polls, new voters joined, and the party won over groups, such as the blacks, who had been Republicans for generations—at first haltingly, then enthusiastically and overwhelmingly. The result was the New Deal coalition that dominated the country for more than 30 years."[2]

"The early Republicans were united in their opposition to extending slavery into the Western territories. In 1856 they nominated John Charles Frémont for the presidency. He won about a third of the popular vote, but alienated many potential supporters by his failure to oppose immigration." [2] The Republicans joined the Democrats as one of the nation's two major parties in the late 1850s. In the early 1860s moderate and radical Republicans quarreled bitterly over their war aims, even as they fought together against their common Democratic enemy. Radicals wanted to use the war to end slavery and, to some degree, reshape the society and power structure of the South. The moderates agreed on the abolition of slavery but rejected the idea of imposing racial equality or attempting to reshape the South's social and economic structure. Republican leaders argued that Whigs and blacks had a common belief in the need for strong government action in society, but these arguments were ineffective in the face of racist campaigns by the Southern Democrats. Support for black rights waned when Republicans perceived that this support was costing the party needed votes, but even this did not help the party in the South, where the blacks were disfranchised and the whites for the most part remained Democratic. Republican state platforms frequently advocated government intervention to prohibit or limit liquor consumption and to shape school curriculum in order to promote certain Protestant and American values against the threats posed by

the newcomers, who became closely allied with the Democratic Party. The Great Depression, which began during Hoover's administration, destroyed America's belief in that dream of unlimited prosperity and its faith in the Republican Party. The disastrous economic collapse and extraordinarily high unemployment that followed made a mockery of Republican claims.

What changed in the last 100 years?

"More people than ever before identified themselves as Democrats." As the party solidified its support among blacks, however, it lost southern whites and northern labor and ethnic voters. The country prospered, but conflicts over social and military policy intensified." [1] The Democrats gained support of Blacks and they were more for the working man while the Republicans were for the businessman. The Northern Democrats became pro Civil Rights. Democrats are suffering an identity crisis because of their all-inclusive stance. They believe that all people are equal and fight for equal rights of all. This internal diversity is what makes decision-making so difficult.

Locations of Party Members

The way to simplify this decision-making process is to be unified in God. There are many Democrats who are Christians and many who are not and the balance is to include all people regardless of religious background has been the challenge to Democrats.

So why become a Democrat? I think many still cling to the party because it is all-inclusive: black, white, poor, common man, Hispanic, African, you name it, the Democrats will accept all people. They generally do not discriminate. It is difficult for people to attach themselves to a party where they feel that they are not equal in pay, hiring, work or wealth. They support Medicare and Medicaid and generally look out for the poor. These programs are in place to assist the unfortunate. Jesus reminds us that there will always be the poor. Why not help them? Yes we need to take care of ourselves but some will not be able to so programs are needed to catch those falling through the cracks. Everyone will not be wealthy although wealth is for everyone. While some have been blessed many others are still living below the poverty line. Make sure that whatever your party is, as a Christian, that you make Jesus your priority and that your motives are based on the Word of God.

The Republican Party has been successful with gaining support from Evangelical Christians. They are standing strong against immoral issues. Still the party fails to connect with the poor and the working class. This will continue to be a challenge as long as programs like Medicare, Medicaid, Affirmative Action and Social Security continue to be a reforming topic for Republicans.

Left Wing Versus Right Wing: What's In A Name

The original term left wing versus right wing originated "from the British House of Commons, where the Popular(Liberal) parties have traditionally sat to the left of the speaker and the Royalist\Aristocratic Parties(Conservative) to the Right." Today this name implies that Democrats or Liberals, live without morality and live freely. Right wing suggests that Republicans are morally correct. Their way is the right way. The other term that is often used is Conservative. Labeling is a powerful tool. These labels can sway a vote because of the connotation. Be sure you know the candidate, not the label only.

Blue State Versus Red State: What's In A Color

During the 2004 Presidential election, a color-coded map was shown on all of the news stations. It showed the red states and the blue states. The red states represented a majority democratic vote and the blue states represented a majority republican vote. This pictorial view of the United States showed that half of the United States stood for morals and the other half was so liberal and free that all they do is sin. The perception is that there is a moral America and an immoral America. So what's in a color? Red states represent a majority Republican view and blue states represent a majority democratic view. http://www-personal.umich.edu/~mejn/election/

Even in the beginning, when the Democratic party split there was a difference of opinion. Our government is setup as a system of checks and balances. There is a two party system: the Democrats with their set of general beliefs and the Republicans with their set of general beliefs. Naturally there will be disagreements but as Christians, we must have fundamental agreements. What are those agreements? First and foremost, we have to believe that Jesus is the Son of God. We must accept and obey the Ten Commandments. We must love one another as Christ loves the Church. After this fundamental foundation has been laid, we can then begin to tackle other issues.

1 Corinthians 1:10 tells us *"Now I plead with you, brethren, by the name of our Lord Jesus Christ, that you all speak the same thing, and that there be no divisions among you, but that you be perfectly joined together in the same mind and in the same judgment"*. Paul told the Church of Corinth that there should be no divisions among them. He asked them if Christ was divided. There should be no strife or contentions amongst Christians. Satan is the root of strife and contention. He wants the Christians Democrats and the Christian Republicans to fight with each other so that nothing gets accomplished. The color codes show the "morality" states.

The Ministers Are Divided? Who's right?

Not only are the Democrats and the Republicans divided, the churches in America are the most divided churches in the world. We have so many denominations and there is the racial divide. It is often said that Sunday morning is the most divided day of the week because we all go off to our denominations and worship with those who are like us.

Just as we disagree about issues today, people disagreed about issues in Biblical times. One such issue was circumcision. There was so much debate over this issue that Acts 15:6-21 talks about the Jerusalem Council. The purpose of the council was to discuss the necessity of circumcision.

> *"And certain men came down from Judea and taught the brethren, "Unless you are circumcised according to the custom of Moses, you cannot be saved." 2 Therefore, when Paul and Barnabas had no small dissension and dispute with them, they determined that Paul and Barnabas and certain others of them should go up to Jerusalem, to the apostles and elders, about this question." (Acts 15:1-2)*

The question the author posed in Step by Step of the New Testament is "Must the Gentiles Adopt Jewish Lifestyle? Some Christian Pharisees insisted that Gentiles needed to submit to circumcision and obey Mosaic laws (laws of Moses) [5]. Peter told them about his experience with Cornelius. Acts 10:1-2 describes Cornelius.

There was a certain man in Caesarea called Cornelius, a centurion of what was called the Italian Regiment, 2 a devout *man* and one who feared God with all his household, who gave alms generously to the people, and prayed to God always.

Cornelius, the Gentile, was a man of God. An angel of the Lord came to Cornelius in a vision and told him to send for Peter (Acts 10:5). God then gave Peter a vision. **Acts 10:9-15** describes Peter's vision.

The next day, as they went on their journey and drew near the city, Peter went up on the housetop to pray, about the sixth hour. Then he became very hungry and wanted to eat; but while they made ready, he fell into a trance and saw heaven opened and an object like a great sheet bound at the four corners, descending to him and let down to the earth. In it were all kinds of four-footed animals of the earth, wild beasts, creeping things, and birds of the air. And a voice came to him, "Rise, Peter; kill and eat." But Peter said, "Not so, Lord! For I have never eaten anything common or unclean." And a voice *spoke* to him again the second time, "What God has cleansed you must not call common." This was done three times. And the object was taken up into heaven again.

Peter's vision showed all types of animals and wild beasts and God told him to kill and eat. Peter rejected this initially because he had never eaten anything unclean (verse 14). God told him what has been cleansed is not common. This verse shows us that we can have our own doctrine and our own belief that we think is right and true but if we be sensitive to the Spirit of God, pray and stay in the Word, he will correct our thinking. He will tell you what's right or wrong doctrine. This vision was necessary because God had to prepare Peter's heart to witness to the Gentile. Peter had to experience this for himself so that when he went to the Jerusalem Council, they would not reject what God had given him. They would not hold the Gentiles to the Mosaic law. See verses 18-21 below.

Known to God from eternity are all His works. Therefore, I judge that we should not trouble those from among the Gentiles who are turning to God, but that we write to them to abstain from things polluted by idols, *from* sexual immorality, *from* things strangled, and *from* blood. For Moses has had throughout many generations those who preach him in every city, being read in the synagogues every Sabbath

He encouraged them not to hold the Gentiles to the law of circumcision but tell them to abstain from things polluted by idols, from sexual immorality, from things strangled and from blood. I use this example to show how a very important issue was resolved in Biblical times. We can be divided on issues without Biblical reasoning. Some issues should not be debatable: taking care of the poor and needy, salvation, love, healthcare, morality, sin, education, and peace.

We can all get along. We should all agree on the Word and work to resolve other issues that may come up. We should not be so lopsided that we become detached from Jesus, the true vine.

During the 2004 and 2008 election, Ministers became an integral part of the elections. Politicians were visiting churches as they usually do and encourage church members to vote. The politicians stated their cases and discussed their platform. They told the church why they should vote for them. Politicians encouraged the ministers to encourage their members to get out and vote. It was a great grassroots campaign and a strategic plan to capture more votes. Many ministers chose sides. Some supported the Democratic ticket and many the Republican ticket indirectly. I say indirectly because if you are a 501c3 organization, it is unlawful to support a party as an organization. You could loose your 501c3 status. Both parties had very important issues. So the question is, who is right? Well the basic answer is what does the word of God say. We cannot be blinded by a minister or political figure because the Word of God says all have fallen short of the glory of God. They are subject to make mistakes. We have to check their views against the word of God. If Minister A believes in helping the poor and needy and Minster B is against abortion, which do you support? You would support ministers A and B, right. Now let's dig a little deeper. Suppose Minister A supported helping the poor and needy but for a woman's right to choose. Should we then support Minister A? You have to seek God. Make sure the people that you are following are of God and are following the Word of God. The Word says that we are to work out our own salvation. Meaning, I am responsible for my own salvation. You can not make my choices for me and I can not make them for you. We will be held responsible for our individual choices. Therefore, WE are responsible for checking the Word of God for ourselves.

Recently one church kicked their members out because they voted for the Democratic Presidential candidate. This is not balanced and this is not of God. God still loves us regardless of how we voted. [6] This was an extreme case.

To The Ministers

Ministers, you are very influential in the choices we make. We rely on you to go to the Word of God and tell us what "thus says the Lord" not thus says you. Since many members will not do the research and read the Word for themselves, it is imperative that you preach what God says. The members are depending on you for direction. While it is illegal for a church to endorse a political party, individually, members will approach you about who they should vote for. A voting guideline is available at the end of the book to assist you because there are so many candidates with a vast array of views. There are some who appear to be right but we must check their voting record. Seek God and ask him who you should vote for. When you stick to the Word of God, it is then that members' responsibility to take that information and seek God for themselves. There are flaws in all candidates. Whatever your personal party affiliation is, look past the party and look at the candidate. As a minister, do not endorse the candidate because he/she is a Republican or a Democrat. See what their motives are and the voting record. Vote in support of the Word of God! I believe God is tearing down party lines and walls. The line that divides the

Democrats from the Republicans will be moved and their will be new parties emerging, a Christian party. Where will they sit? How will it be designed?

I believe the new design will look like it is today. They may sit on the Democratic or Republican side but they will be Christians. In the State of Union address when the President speaks, whoever the party leader is at that time, the winning group stands up and claps when something is said that resonates in their spirit. If A Democratic President is in office, when the Democratic President says something, all the Democrats on the left-side stand up and clap while the Republicans sit down in unified disagreement. When the Republican President is in office, the Republicans stand and cheer when the President makes his statements while the Democrats sit down unified in their disagreement. I believe a day is coming when ALL CHRISTIANS will stand when the leader speaks what is right in God's eyes. These Christians will be on both sides. Those who are sitting down will be those do not know God. I believe party affiliation will not longer be a barrier to allowing God's laws to manifest. I believe that political Christians will vote their conscience instead of voting to stay in office. The will of God will be more important than their own personal agenda. The ministers may be divided now but I believe that the real men and women of God will begin to stand up for what is right and their will be no division but unity in Christ Jesus. No one will be divided on God's word. We will have the guts to look the devil in the face and tell him that we will no longer give into his sly tactics. We will no longer allow him to use our vote to sin against the will of God. We will stand up for what is right. God's will is of the up most importance. We will hold these public officers accountable especially if they say they are of God. So let's dig in the word, find the supporting scripture and vote the way God leads us. Do not vote in support of tradition. Let us not be blinded by either party.

During the 2004 Presidential election, many Christians supported George W. Bush and many supported John Kerry. Their names are worth mentioning because this election came down to morals. President Bush professed his Christianity to the world. People who voted against Bush were made to feel that they were not of God. Today, it is Donald Trump and Hillary Clinton. The ministers were divided. If the ministers were divided, then just think about all the confused Christians running around without clear guidance. I was one of them. Everyone stated their cases and found supporting scripture to back it up. We should trust God and seek direction from the Holy Spirit and trust God to do the rest.

My plea is please do not be deceived by men and make your decisions on what they say. Look for balanced leaders who stand on the Word of God. Look for the Christian Democrat, the Christian Republican or the Christian Independent who is balanced and not left-winged or right-winged. Look for those who are relying on God and who love all people and focus on all issues not just one or two.

Growing Morally Questions
Do I have an alt with my brother?
Will I allow the Holy Spirit to guide me?
Am I willing to work across the aisle with my Christian brother or sister?

Prayer

Lord while there have been many disagreements since the beginning of time, You have always provided avenues of reconciliation. Give us wisdom on how to settle matters. Do not let us bash each other or walk in discord. Lord you said where to or three are gathered, there You are in the midst. Help us to walk in Your wise counsel and dwell together in unity. Even though there are differences of opinions, laws and aisles separating us, help to bridge those differences with Your love and seek You for guidance on the issues in Jesus name.

Biblical References – Moral Checkup

For by one Spirit we were all baptized into one body— whether Jews or Greeks, whether slaves or free—and have all been made to drink into one Spirit. For in fact the body is not one member but many. 1 Corinthians 12:13-14

Finally, brethren, farewell. Become complete. Be of good comfort, be of one mind, live in peace; and the God of love and peace will be with you. 2 Corinthians 13:11

Behold, how good and how pleasant it is for brethren to dwell together in unity! Psalm 133:1

I, therefore, the prisoner of the Lord, beseech you to walk worthy of the calling with which you were called, with all lowliness and gentleness, with longsuffering, bearing with one another in love, endeavoring to keep the unity of the Spirit in the bond of peace. Ephesians 4:1-3

Be kindly affectionate to one another with brotherly love, in honor giving preference to one another; not lagging in diligence, fervent in spirit, serving the Lord; rejoicing in hope, patient in tribulation, continuing steadfastly in prayer; distributing to the needs of the saints, given to hospitality. Romans 10:12-13

If it is possible, as much as depends on you, live peaceably with all men. Romans 12:8

Chapter Eleven

Can We All
Just Get Along!

"How good and pleasant it is when God's people live together in unity" (Psalm 133.1).

"Can we all just get along" are the famous words of Rodney King, a man who was beaten during the Los Angeles race riots. While there have been many jokes about this famous line, the reason for the popularity is because it resonates with all people. If I am a Christian Republican or I am a Christian Democrat, because we are Christians, should we all be able to get along? Jesus encourages us to dwell together in unity. We become divisive because we believe our issue is more important than another or we disagree with someone else's way of thinking. We must establish what we are to agree on. For Christians, the first and foremost issue we should agree upon is Jesus is the Son of God. He died on the cross for our sins. In order to be restored back to our Father, we have to repent of our sins and accept Jesus as our personal Savior. While there are Christians who are divided along party lines, they are still people who have accepted the Lord as their personal savior. Many feel strongly about one issue versus another. Many are against abortion and disapprove of Roe vs. Wade (the law that made abortion legal). Many believe God is more concerned about taking care of the poor and needy and this causes the division. We must be careful and not to loose focus of what is important, the gift of salvation and truly representing Christ. While one party may emphasize one issue more than another, if you are a Christian, you must first be reconciled to Christ and His Word. How do you do this? Well if you have accepted Jesus as your personal savior, you are reconciled to Christ. Now that we have the common ground established, we can continue on our reconciliation path. 2 Corinthians 5:18 reminds us that:

All things are of God, who has reconciled us to Himself through Jesus Christ, and has given us the ministry of reconciliation, [19] that is, that God was in Christ reconciling the world to Himself, not imputing their trespasses to them, and has committed to us the word of reconciliation. 2 Corinthians 5:18-19

When we are reconciled to Christ, we have the Holy Spirit who will guide us into all truth (John 16:13). Putting a label on you does not fully describe who you are. Saying I am American does not fully describe me. Saying I am woman does not fully describe me. Saying I am a Christian and a servant of God is the way I would prefer to be described. While we have our discussions on the issues we feel should be at the forefront, we must have Christ as our foundation. Jesus criticized the Pharisees for ignoring the **weightier matters such as justice, mercy and faithfulness (Matthew 23:23)**. He still expected them to pay their tithes. He said continue to do both not emphasize one over the other.

All of these issues are important and when there is any discussion, there will be disagreements but what we must always agree on first and foremost is that all of the Word of God is true. We must then take the issue that we are discussing and judge it against the Word of God. Here are some ways to judge the issue according to the Word of God.

✓ Does the issue go against the Word of God?
✓ Does the issue hurt the people involved?

✓ Does the issue exclude the people involved?

We have to be sure that we are advancing God's message and not our own. What are our motives? We cannot use Christ as a banner and not follow all of His Word completely. Abortion is important, taking care of the poor and needy is important. Justice and fairness to all is important. We, the Christian Republican and the Christian Democrat, are guilty for using one issue as a platform to run on. We need to look at all issues. We must be balanced. When we push our issue to the forefront, we run the risk of excluding others. We have to be just and examine all. God is watching all of us. If I say I am against abortion but I turn my back on my brother or sister when they are hungry, I have still sinned. While we have our causes, my cause is not more important than your cause. They are equally important. Remember no sin is greater. Let us examine ourselves against God's Word. Let us examine our motives against God's Word. Let us be careful to check the spirits of those who run for office. Let us check the motives. The book of Hosea says "my people suffer for lack of knowledge". God did not create us to be ignorant or remain ignorant. He created us to be knowledgeable of ALL of His Word. We are to apply this Word to our lives and share it with those around us. We are to change the environment in which we live by sharing this powerful, unadulterated Word. ALL OF IT!

Division is seen in the Congress and Senate today. They are portrayed as being fruitless. They have sessions and they are not able to vote on certain laws before they go on summer break. They fight for laws but become deadlocked. Isaiah 55:8 states that God's thoughts are not our thoughts, neither are His ways our ways". In **Experiencing God** (Blackaby, King, pg. 81-81), the authors state

His (God's) goal is to reveal Himself to people to draw them into a love relationship with Himself. His ways are

redemptive. He acts in such a way to reveal Himself and His love. He does not simply wait around in order to help us achieve our goals for Him! He comes to accomplish His own goals through us – and in His own way". The authors go on to say "God does not work in man's ways. We will not accomplish God's work in our own ways...Our ways may seem good to us. We may accomplish some moderate successes. When we try to do the work of God in our own ways, however, we will never see the mighty power of God in what we do. God reveals His ways because this is the only way to accomplish His purposes. When God accomplishes His purposes, His ways through us, people will come to know God. They will recognize that what has happened can only be explained by God. He will get the glory Himself.

Many in the Congress and Senate come to office with the wrong agenda, their own agenda. Many are not saved and many do not seek God before they make decisions. We should expect to fight against the world because we are of Christ and Satan is Christ's arch enemy, but within Christ, we should have unity. If we were to do it God's way, we could accomplish so much more with just a little. Jesus did this when He fed the multitude of people with 5 loaves of bread and 2 fish. Since Jesus depended on God, God was able to take the little amount and do greater works because Jesus surrendered to God. If we would only surrender to God with what we have, our talents, our money or our time, God could multiply and do so much more. Even though the Senate and the Congressmen only meet during certain seasons of the year, if they would yield to the Holy Spirit because the "Holy Spirit knows the mind of God" [1],

God would speak to them and they would accomplish so much more.

We should pray before we vote. *Romans 8:26-27 tells us:*

Likewise the Spirit also helps in our weaknesses. For we do not know what we should pray for as we ought, but the Spirit Himself makes intercession for us with groanings which cannot be uttered. Now He who searches the hearts knows what the mind of the Spirit is, because He makes intercession for the saints according to the will of God.

The Holy Spirit makes intercession for God's people to do the will of God. **John 16:13** states *"He will not speak on his own; he will speak only what he hears, and he will tell you what is yet to come".* If we would only seek Him, He will tell us what is yet to come. He will tell us about wars, terrorists' plots, and storms but we only know this by having a relationship with Him. In order to pray we need to have a relationship with God, we have to seek God's face daily. We should not approach God when we have problems only but we are to enter into a love relationship with God. Those of us who continue to struggle in areas that are not pleasing to God should seek His face daily and the Holy Spirit will speak to us and strengthen so we will be delivered. The Holy Spirit will guide us into all truth. He has the highest wisdom and that wisdom is from God Almighty and our God will never lead us astray. Pray and seek His face before you make a decision about a law. Ask God, what do you want to happen? How will You use me? How do You want me to vote? What is Your will not my will? Yes, you may get backlash from others but as long You have done the will of God. He will say well done my good and faithful servant.

You are a servant of God, Christian President, Christian Congressman, Christian Senator, Christian public official. Submit to

His will and His ways. Vote no to abortion. Vote yes to helping those in need. Vote yes to equal treatment of all people. Vote yes to justice, mercy and peace. Vote yes to defend God's people. Vote yes to help third world countries who need our help. Let your heart be full of mercy, justice and peace. Let your heart be full of the Word of God so You will have the wisdom of God.

> **But God has revealed them to us through His Spirit. For the Spirit searches all things, yes, the deep things of God. For what man knows the things of a man except the spirit of the man which is in him? Even so no one knows the things of God except the Spirit of God. Now we have received, not the spirit of the world, but the Spirit who is from God, that we might know the things that have been freely given to us by God." 1 Corinthians 2:10-12**

Christians should not have the spirit of the world but the spirit of God.

God is calling the Christian Democrat, the Christian Republican, the Independent and every other Christian party affiliate to unify in His word. This means that you can vote no to abortion as a Democrat. This means that you can vote yes to helping the poor and the needy if you are a Republican. This means you can vote yes to justice, mercy, and peace regardless of what side of the aisle you sit on. Vote yes to Jesus and acknowledge Him in all your ways and He will direct your path. There are characteristics from both parties that are beneficial and if we become united on these issues, this world could be transformed. Moral Issues (The Ten Commandments), loving each other as Christ loved the church, caring for the poor, staying away from greed, civil rights and equal treatment of all men and women. I will only accentuate the positive from both sides because this is what is needed for true reconciliation.

Paul speaks of unity and diversity in one body in 1 Corinthians 1:12:24-26.

> *While our presentable parts need no special treatment.*
> *But God has combined the members of the body and has*
> *given greater honor to the parts that lacked it, so that*
> *there should be no division in the body, but that its parts*
> *should have equal concern for each other. If one part*
> *suffers, every part suffers with it; if one part is honored,*
> *every part rejoices with it."*

While there are many members and all have many functions, all are needed. While there are many issues and many causes that are good, they should all be considered and all are needed. Diversity does not mean discord unless we choose to see it that way. The most diverse group in the Bible was Jesus' disciples. They came from all backgrounds and Jesus used them anyway. They were on one accord with Jesus and got more accomplished.

While we may disagree on issues that are important, we must remember to keep what is important to God. We must NOT limit the Word of God and have selective platforms. Our full platform should represent the Word of God in its entirety!

Growing Morally Questions
Do I have a Spirit of Reconciliation?
Will I allow the Holy Spirit to guide me?
Am I willing to work across the aisle with my Christian brother or sister?

Prayer

Lord please give us the spirit of reconciliation. Lord You are the perfect example of reconciliation since You have reconciled us back to the Father by accepting us. Your blood has washed away our sins. Your love binds us together and no issue or law can keep us from serving You. I thank you for love, mercy, justice and faithfulness in Jesus' name. Amen.

Biblical References – Moral Checkup

All things are of God, who has reconciled us to Himself through Jesus Christ, and has given us the ministry of reconciliation, that is, that God was in Christ reconciling the world to Himself, not imputing their trespasses to them, and has committed to us the word of reconciliation. 2 Corinthians 5:18-19

If the world hates you, you know that it hated Me before it hated you. If you were of the world, the world would love its own. Yet because you are not of the world, but I chose you out of the world, therefore the world hates you. John 15:18-19

There are different kinds of gifts, but the same Spirit. There are different kinds of service, but the same Lord. There are different kinds of working, but the same God works all of them in all men. 1 Corinthians 12:4-6

The body is a unit, though it is made up of many parts; and though all its parts are many, they form one body. So it is with Christ. For we were all baptized by one Spirit into one body—whether Jews or Greeks, slave or free—and we were all given the one Spirit to drink. 1 Corinthians 12:12-13

But all these things they will do to you for My name's sake, because they do not know Him who sent Me. John 15:21

They will put you out of the synagogues; yes, the time is coming that whoever kills you will think that he offers God service. And these things they will do to you because they have not known the Father nor Me. John 16:2-3

Only let your conduct be worthy of the gospel of Christ, so that whether I come and see you or am absent, I may hear of your affairs, that you stand fast in one spirit, with one mind striving together for the faith of the gospel Philippians 1:27

Chapter Twelve

Why Do Most African-Americans Vote For Democrats?

"Know therefore that the LORD thy God, he is God, the faithful God, which keepeth covenant and mercy with them that love him and keep his commandments to a thousand generations" (Deuteronomy 7:9).

African-Americans are the most evolving group of people in the United States. This is a group that has struggled with their identity since they were brought over to the United States 200 years ago. When we were brought over from our native country Africa, we were enslaved and stripped of all pride. We were taught to be totally submissive to our earthly masters. Now you have a people who were sold into slavery, told what to do on a daily basis, beaten, raped, lynched, and emotionally abused. You have this people who have come to this country founded by Christopher Columbus with its own laws and its own structure. They were taught submission and it was a forced submission. We were given a derogatory name. This is not a message to bring up old issues or to bash the Caucasian race but to show you why there is a loyalty to the Democratic Party. Webster's definition of the "n" word as we call it is "Used as a disparaging term for a Black person".

There is much debate over this word today about who has the right to use it. Many African-Americans use the word loosely to define a brotherhood even though it has derogatory roots. If a white person uses it then it is wrong is what society says. We have to ask the reason why we are using it. If it is meant to be derogatory then it should be off limits. It is a double-standard for some to use the word and for others not to use the word. The NAACP had a funeral service for the word as a symbolic gesture that the African-American race should denounce the word. I can see how people would try to make something positive out of something negative but if we know it offends someone, be respectful enough not use it. This applies to words that would degrade other races outside of the African-American race.

The second definition I found is what really surprised me. It states that it is "used as a disparaging term for a member of any socially, economically, or politically deprived group of people". It says that this new class of people was socially, economically and politically deprived people. Now when you are socially deprived it means that you do not have the luxury of participating in the good things of life. When we think of a social, we think of people interacting in a fun and enjoyable environment. I am reminded of the story of Cinderella. She was not allowed to go to the ball, she was deprived socially. She had to get her stepmother and her stepsisters dressed to go. She helped them participate in their social lifestyle but she was deprived much like the dark-skinned people of that time. We were deprived socially and economically. This simply means that these people worked for free. They were given food but worked from sun up to sun down for free. They did not have any assets. They did not own anything, they only had each other so they became dependent on each other. They learned to survive. This is why you can put these dark-skinned people in any environment today and they can survive because they were built to survive. This is why when these dark-skinned people were given the scraps of the pig, they could still make a meal out of leftovers like neck bones, pigtails and oxtails. We now know these things lead to high-blood pressure but before that is all we had to work with. This is another example of taking something negative and trying to make it positive.

Now the last way that we were deprived was politically. These dark-skinned people were not allowed to vote. They did not have a voice. They only had the choice to follow the law but not participate in the creating of the laws. These people were deprived socially, economically and politically. These people were beaten and killed without remorse by a group of hateful. The system was setup in such a way that white people were superior and black people were inferior.

My Great Grandmother – A Slave

My Great-grandmother, "Dear Heart", told us of a story of when she used to pick cotton. She was 5 feet tall and 95 pounds. She said that she used to pick about 500 to 600 pounds per day from sun up to sun down. She was sick and tired one day and she was not able to pick the cotton as fast as usual. She said her overseer whom she called "Master" told her that she needed to speed it up. She told him she did not feel well and could not move much faster. He was angry and did to accept this. He came back to her and told her to speed it up again and she had the same response. In his anger, he picked up a hatchet and hit her in the head. She had blood coming down all over her. She had to bandage herself up because he left her to die. She healed on her own with the help of God and still had to return to work for him. She used to show us the imprint in the top, middle of her head of gray hair. She went on to be with the Lord when she was 110.

Even though all of these things happened, God still had a remnant of people who loved Him and knew it was wrong. He used pilgrims who were white and others to help blacks. Blacks got together and used the same Constitution that white men created to say that all men were created equal to prove their case that they too were a part of all men. Men with consciences listened and because they were of God and hearts changed. I know other motives came into play but the bottom line is God still changed the heart of His people. Jesus said, my sheep know my voice. President Lincoln signed the Emancipation Proclamation to free the slaves despite the opposition of the South.

Now comes the first phase of the evolution. The people are starting to have an awakening. They no longer want to be called the "n" word but now they are called the Negro. The new name Negro would give us more pride. It would remove us from the negative connotations of the "n" word. So now we have this new word to help us move into our new identity. With this new word we have hope. We are not slaves anymore. We had a voice. We could vote. Initially our vote only counted as only three-fifths because slaves were counted as three-fifths of a person.

We did not stay Negroes long because the name still had ties to the "N" word. Then came the name Afro-American. This would connect us back to our roots and show that we are not just Americans but descendants from a far land. Lastly, the name African-American evolved. This name would show the split between two countries. So now these dark-skinned people, myself included, are now proudly African-Americans. Now during these times of identity uncertainty, God used many people to help African-Americans. These people were God's elite. They were the Christian people. These people invested in African-Americans by teaching them how to read, showing them favor and standing with Blacks to change the system. During this time of change God raised up mighty men to defend the rights of this deprived people. Martin Luther King, Jr. had the courage to fight for equal rights. His example of non-violence was the mirror image of Christ's way. He chose to have a non-violent and non-retaliatory defense to racism. People spat on him and beat him because they disagreed with him standing up for a deprived people. His boldness in the face of racism, oppression and exclusion led to the Civil Rights movement. He was a leading Democrat. He was a minister of the gospel of Jesus Christ. Others fought for Civil Rights and against injustice such as Representative John Lewis, Rev. Jessie Jackson, Rev. Dr. A. H. Hoffman, *my husband's grandfather*, Harry Belefonte, Rev. Al Sharpton, Richard Allen, President John F. Kennedy, Nelson Mandela, Malcolm X, Peter Singer, Julian Bond, John Marshall Harlan, Frederick Douglass, Hank Aaron, Stokely Carmichael, Jim Clyburn, Vernon Jordan, Jr., Barbara Jordan, Barack Obama, Michelle Obama, Andrew Young, Ralph D. Abernathy, Ruby Bridges, etc. and so many other African-Americans and Caucasians a Democrat? Why were John Fitzgerald Kennedy and Ted Kennedy a Democrat? Why did they identify with this party more than the Republican Party? This is the party that showed concerned, cared and acted on the Black communities' behalf. Mennonites and Quakers were people who opposed slavery in the late 17th century. God even used more Christian ministers to oppose slavery and discrimination of Blacks.

My Mother – Civil Rights Activist

In Supreme Court Case of the United States, No. 80-2100, my mother, Gloria Sullivan, alongside of Mr. Herman Lodge, fought for civil rights. They fought to have Burke County, Georgia split up into wards. The Fourteenth Amendment rights of Burke County's black citizens.

My mother was also active in the Civil Rights movement. She worked with Herman Lodge to fight discrimination in Waynesboro, Georgia. Also, she was discriminated against at the local Laundromat in Waynesboro, Georgia. The owner told her, "you can't read the sign? It says private and that means colored people can't use this washhouse. He said why can't y'all colored people act the way y'all used to? If you don't get those clothes out of here, you'll see what happens to you". She was told to leave (UPI, 1980). She fought against this discrimination and also won.

Black Republicans

In doing my research, I found out that when the political parties were just created, it was Republicans that fought against slavery. This also caused me to go back and look at history because I had never heard this before. What happened in the last 100 years to make Black America switch parties?

"In 1870, another Civil Rights Act was passed, and was immediately followed by the 15th Amendment - *"the right of citizens of the United States to vote shall not be denied or abridged by the United States or by any State on account of race, color or previous conditions of servitude."* [1]

At the start of Reconstruction, nearly 90% of Blacks lived in the South. As a result of 15th amendment, many Blacks were elected to prominent offices in the South.

Seventeen Blacks were elected to serve in the U. S. House of Representatives and the U. S. Senate. Blanche K. Bruce and Hiram Revels from Mississippi were the first Blacks to be elected to the U.S. senate. Bruce served a full term, while Revels only served a year and a half. All of these elected officials were Republicans. As a matter of fact, 80% of the Republican voters in the South were Black men."

In the beginning most blacks were Republicans but they moved away from the party. In Oscar Eason Jr.'s article *Why blacks shy away from the* GOP, he points out:

> *"Anyone who is politically curious has seen present-day Republican pundits proclaim their party to be historically "the party of Lincoln"; what is unfailingly left out of this declaration is the historical*

metamorphosis of the Republican Party after Reconstruction. Anyone who does not understand this genealogy cannot hope to understand the predominately white face of today's GOP." [2]

"In the late 1940s President Truman, a Democrat, decided it was time to racially integrate the armed forces, causing outrage among some white Southern Democrats. As if this were not enough, in 1948 the Democratic Party publicly declared its support for the civil rights movement. That was more than some white Southern Democrats could stomach, so they formed a "states rights" ticket that was appropriately labeled the Dixiecrats." [2]

"In the mid 1960s, the Dixicrats switched from the Democratic to the Republican Party to assist Barry Goldwater in his unsuccessful bid for the presidency against Lyndon Johnson. They were, however, pivotal in the Southern strategy that won the White House for Richard M. Nixon in 1968. President Reagan, a Republican, is credited with bringing all factions of the Republican right-wing conservative movement together, steeped in the Dixiecrat states' rights tradition." [2]

"During Reagan's administration, the issues and concerns of the Dixiecrats became principally those of the Republican Party. It was precisely at this juncture that the Republican Party ceased being the Party of Lincoln and evolved into what it is today to the vast majority of black America -- almost racially exclusive and dedicated to protecting and maintaining the status quo. In this context, it is difficult to imagine how the

average civil rights-sensitive black citizen could blend in to today's Republican Party." [2]

During the Civil Rights movement, there was so much hate and animosity during this era. There was a campaign to keep Blacks from voting. President Kennedy urged people to treat people equal regardless of race or color. President Lyndon Johnson signed the Voting Rights Act of 1964. The allegiance to the Democratic Party was formed because the government was finally hearing the voice of Blacks. President Kennedy marched with Blacks and supported equal treatment of Blacks. This allegiance was formed because we had someone to stand up for us. Social programs were put in place to help the poor. Attention was given to the neglected, the underrepresented and the needy. Most of the people that fit into this category were Blacks.

Today, racism still exists but not as it did in the past. God has moved on our behalf and has opened doors for us. Affirmative Action has also leveled the playing field. I know many do not agree that it is fair but being an African-American in corporate America, I have seen first hand the lack of Diversity in leadership roles. Many companies are becoming more progressive and changes are being made. Diversity has become a key issue. Corporations are realizing that dollars are made by diverse people which means they also have the power to choose where they will spend their money. Also, colleges such as the University of Phoenix and Claflin University are making access to education to all people. If it were not for Affirmative Action many people would not have been hired at all. The law was necessary because it forces corporate America to balance the playing field. Many companies are doing the right thing and it is not needed as much as it has been.

There are still issues with equal pay. Many Black men are paid on a lower salary scale than white males. This is why there is an increase in the number of African-American small business owners. They are not able to move to the top of the Corporate America so they become their own bosses. One of my prayers is that the Christian men and women in corporate America will step up and let go of their prejudices and be fair, not in word but in action.

Black Republican

There are many African-Americans who are have come out of the political closet. They are the Black Republican. The Ohio GOP has this statement on its board:

"Our party is continuing that legacy by addressing the issues of importance to African American communities: lower taxes, public safety, school choice, faith-based charity, health care and equal opportunity. The Ohio Republican Party's Campaign America program is designed to promote these agendas to minority constituencies and recruit qualified Republican minorities to run for public office." 3

The Republican Party is also reaching out to African-Americans. President George W. Bush had the most diverse cabinet in the history. Some are switching to this party because it represents their views today. Many African-Americans are prosperous and have "made it". They are also open about their faith. They feel the Republican Party represents who they are today as opposed to whom they were.

African Americans Working With
The Republicans and The Democrats

Both parties have been responsible for helping African-Americans. First, God used the Republicans to stand against slavery. Secondly, God used the Democrats to fight for Civil Rights. Both had a part in our destiny. God has freed all of His people from bondage. He is calling us to forgive and walk together in unity regardless of race or color. We can be passionate about issues but we must go to the Word and seek God for guidance. I am passionate about justice. I speak up against unfair treatment of people. Seek God in prayer and trust the Holy Spirit's leading on what we should do. Do it in love with the boldness of Christ.

The African American journey can be likened to the journey of the Israelites. God used Moses to deliver the Israelites and Joshua took them into the Promised Land. God used Blacks and Whites to help African-Americans but He raised up a leader who fought back based on the word of God. He was Martin Luther King, Jr. Rev. King had a dream.

I Have a Dream – By Dr. Martin Luther King, Jr.

I have a dream that one day this nation will rise up and live out the true meaning of its creed: "We hold these truths to be self-evident: that all men are created equal." I have a dream that one day on the red hills of Georgia the sons of former slaves and the sons of former slave-owners will be able to sit down together at a table of brotherhood. I have a dream that one day even the state of Mississippi, a desert state, sweltering with the heat of injustice and oppression, will be transformed into an oasis of freedom and justice. I have a dream that my four children will one day live in a nation where they will not be judged by the color of their skin but by the content of their character. I have a dream today.

I have a dream that one day the state of Alabama, whose governor's lips are presently dripping with the words of interposition and nullification, will be transformed into a situation where little black boys and black girls will be able to join hands with little white boys and white girls and walk together as sisters and brothers. I have a dream today. I have a dream that one day every valley shall be exalted, every hill and mountain shall be made low, the rough places will be made plain, and the crooked places will be made straight, and the glory of the Lord shall be revealed, and all flesh shall see it together. This is our hope. This is the faith with which I return to the South. With this faith we will be able to hew out of the mountain of despair a stone of hope. With this faith we will be able to transform the jangling discords of our nation into a beautiful symphony of brotherhood. With this faith we will be able to work together, to pray together, to struggle together, to go to jail together, to stand up for freedom together, knowing that we will be free one day." [4]

Dr. Martin Luther King's dream came true. We are able to mingle, play and socialize with a person regardless of race. There is still work to do, but major strides have been made.

We are Free!

To all of my brothers and sisters in Christ today of all races, I would like to say that we are free. I know the law says that man's law says we are free. I am talking about spiritual law. Jesus died on the cross for our sins so that we could be free. This freedom is better than any law that man could create. God wants us to come back to Him. Our lives can be paralleled to the children of Israel. They were in bondage and God raised up Moses and Joshua to deliver them. The Promised Land was right there and they roamed around in the wilderness for forty years. We are still in bondage mentally. This is not just African-Americans but all Americans who have chosen not to accept what God has for them. You are in bondage to Satan if you have not accepted Jesus as your personal savior. We are in slave to sin, if we are still allowing Satan to defeat us in areas that we struggle with.

We have many Joshuas today including Rev. King's wife, Mrs. Coretta Scott King, his daughter Rev. Bernice A. King and the members who lead America and preach to diverse congregations. God is using His people to keep us from going back into bondage to slavery: financial bondage, spiritual bondage, physical bondage and emotional bondage.

Bishop Thomas Weeks III discusses in his book, **Even As Your Soul Prospers,** the laws to unlock the door to an abundant life. This is for all of God's people and is not limited to African-Americans. While the African-American life can be parallel to Israel, anyone who has been in bondage mentally, financially, physically or spiritually can relate to the children of Israel's exodus. There are five laws to live an abundant life regardless of your past. According to him they are:

- Genesis – The Law of Creation
- Exodus – The Law of Expansion
- Leviticus- The Law of Divine Order
- Numbers – The Law of Accountability
- Deuteronomy – The Law of Increase and Overflow [5]

God created us in His image. While we were in bondage to Pharaoh, God used Moses, the Deliverer to bring them children of

Israel out of bondage. He used Joshua to take them to the Promised Land, the land of abundance and expansion. Because there was no order, the Law of Divine order was set in Leviticus. God wanted us to be accountable and He showed this in the Book of Numbers. He brought to Deuteronomy, the Law of Increase and Overflow to bless them.

When God delivered the Israelites, He warned them not to make any other God's before Him. This word was for all people. We have made money, material possessions and organizations our God. We have made idols our god. We are degrading women in our videos and women are accepting it. We still have trouble with other races. Our focus should be on being used by God and not fame or fortune.

When the recording artists get up and thank God for their awards, they have the right order in mind but they also need to match their lives with the Word. They know that God created all things and God has given them ability to get wealth and has given them the talents but this is where they stop short. The other part of this is that God wants their heart. Many recording artists are saved but many are not. They are the ones who have not accepted the Lord as their personal savior. They have been trained by their grandparents to thank God and give God the glory and the honor but they have not really given their lives to God. It is more of a ritual to say "I want to thank God". God also wants your heart. You really do not belong to God if you have not accepted Jesus as your personal savior. We can see this in John 14:21 "Whoever has my commands and obeys them, he is the one who loves me. He who loves me will be loved by my Father, and I too will love him and show myself to him."

Deuteronomy 8:17 tells us that man says *"My power and the might of my hand have gained me this wealth"* and **Deuteronomy 8:18** corrects us and tells that *"You shall remember the Lord your*

God, for it is He who gives you the power to get wealth, that He may establish His covenant which He swore to your fathers, as it is this day".

Many are claiming to be of God and He will say depart from me I never knew you **(Matthew 7:21-23)**. As Christians we have to know that if a person is not saved, we cannot expect them to accept Christ's ideals and understand why we think the way we think and why we live the way we live. **1 Corinthians 2:14** tells us;

The man without the Spirit does not accept the things that come from the Spirit of God, for they are foolishness to him, and he cannot understand them, because they are spiritually discerned."

It will not make sense to the world when you tell them that abortion is wrong, racism is wrong, lying is wrong, fornication is wrong, neglecting the poor is wrong, adultery is wrong, or murder is wrong. They do not have the Spirit of God. It is foolishness to them. They cannot understand what the Word of God says because these things are spiritually discerned. So we have to teach them the way. Many desire Christ and we must relate to them and tell them about the fullness of Christ, not just the fact that he is our provider. We have made this a one-way relationship where we are always in the receiving line. We do not want to give back to Christ. We do not want to give our money, our time or our love. We are to minister to Him just as he ministers to us. Jesus said he is the way, the truth and the life **(John 14:6)**. He is the way to heaven. His ways are the way to heaven. He is the truth. He is the life. We should take on His life and not our own. We should model His ways and not our own. This even means that we should stand up for His laws.

Growing Morally Questions
Will I allow the Holy Spirit to guide me in my decision-making?
Will I trust God to show me the heart of each candidate?
Will my allegiance be to God first?

Prayer

Lord, my race has been through a lot. Help us to forgive anyone who has hurt us or our ancestors. Help us to walk into the destiny and purpose You have for us. If stumbling blocks are before us, help us to seek You and trust You for change. Let us stand for righteousness and let our allegiance be to you first and foremost. God you have called us all to unite in Your word and be loyal to You, not our own ideals. Lord, bring healing to all people in Jesus name. Amen.

Biblical References – Moral Checkup

Do not store up for yourselves treasures on earth, where moth and rust destroy, and where thieves break in and steal. Matthew 6:19

My power and the might of my hand have gained me this wealth. You shall remember the Lord your God, for it is He who gives you the power to get wealth,, that He may establish His covenant which He swore to your fathers, as it is this day. Deuteronomy 8:17-18

For the LORD your God is bringing you into a good land—a land with streams and pools of water, with springs flowing in the valleys and hills; a land with wheat and barley, vines and fig trees, pomegranates, olive oil and honey; [9] a land where bread will not be scarce and you will lack nothing; a land where the rocks are iron and you can dig copper out of the hills. Deuteronomy 8:7-8

Chapter Thirteen

God Is Still In Control!

But he who enters by the door is the shepherd of the sheep. To him the doorkeeper opens, and the sheep hear his voice; and he calls his own sheep by name and leads them out. And when he brings out his own sheep, he goes before them; and the sheep follow him, for they know his voice. Yet they will by no means follow a stranger, but will flee from him, for they do not know the voice of strangers. John 10:2-4

Regardless of your party affiliation, are you of God? Will you stand up for righteousness or will you continue to allow the world to make decisions for you while you idly sit by and say nothing. Will you stand up for the Word of God? Are you God's sheep? Will you follow a stranger? Are you committed to the Word of God and everything in it? John 10 says, "my sheep (God's sheep) knows His voice and a stranger they will not follow". Are you following a stranger? According to Webster's Dictionary, a stranger is one who is neither a friend nor an acquaintance. If leaders do not have a relationship with Jesus and if they are not saved, then we are not to follow them. They are neither a friend or an acquaintance. We are to be a light to the dark world and influence this world. We are not to allow this world to influence us.

Whoever has my commands and obeys them, he is the one who loves me. He who loves me will be loved by my Father, and I too will love him and sow myself to him. John 14:21

God uses His people to accomplish His purpose. God is Almighty and he can do anything he wants to do because He is the creator of this universe and everything in it. In the Bible God used His people to accomplish His will. He used Noah to build the ark and start a new family after the world became so wicked (Genesis 6:5-8, Hebrews 11:7). Only eight people were saved after the flood! He used Abraham to instill faith in His people (Hebrews 11:8 – 12). He used Moses to deliver the Israelites from the hand of Pharaoh. He used Mary to give birth to Jesus, our Lord and Savior and He will use you to stand up for righteousness. So while God is in control, he gave control of the earth to His people and He uses His people to accomplish His will.

God allows us to vote for whom we want. If no one voted, then we would not have a democratic society. No one would be in office but we know that is a very extreme instance. God gave us the authority to govern ourselves on earth. He also gave us a free will to serve him. We have the ability to set laws and create legislation to govern us. Many laws are created out of a need for change or a remedy to a situation. Laws are put in place to protect us from crime, to keep children safe and to protect the elderly. We have a chance to create a government based on our own values and views. The Holy Spirit convicts our heart and leads us so we can make the right decisions that will benefit the society we live in. We express those decisions in the form of a vote.

Joyce Meyer gave a good example of this very subject. She said that her husband Dave was watching Kenneth Copeland she thinks and he said he was getting ready to vote but God told him the person who was going to win was not the person he was going to vote for. He Said God why vote if my person is not going to win. He said because your vote is your seed. A seed is something that is planted to bring about a harvest of that which was planted. If you want a government that reflects God, you plant your seed (your vote)!

God is in control and He knows all. He has all power and He is everywhere, His sheep hear His voice. They are ready to act as the Holy Spirit leads. They are ready to move when He says move. They are ready to say what He tells them to say. They are ready to do what He tells them to do. In **Experiencing God**, there are seven realities of experiencing God. John 5:17, 19-20 Jesus says "My Father is always at His work to this very day, and I, too am working. I tell you the truth, the Son can do nothing by himself; he can do only what he sees the Father is doing, because whatever the Father does the Son also does. For the Father loves the Son, and shows him all he does. Yes, to your amazement he will show him even greater things than these".

Taken from **Experiencing God.**

Jesus' Example:
- The Father has been working right up until now
- Now God has Me working
- I do nothing on My own initiative
- I watch to see what the Father is doing
- I can do what I see the Father is already doing
- You see, the Father loves Me
- He shows Me everything that He, Himself, is doing

The Seven Realities Are Used to Personalize This:

1. God is always at work around you.
2. God pursues a continuing love relationship with you that is real and personal.
3. God invites you to become involved with Him in His work.

4. God speaks by the Holy Spirit through the Bible, prayer, circumstances, and the church to reveal Himself, His purposes and His ways.
5. God's invitation to work with Him always leads you to a crisis of belief that requires faith and action.
6. You must make major adjustments in your life to join God in what He is doing.
7. You come to know God by experience as you obey Him and He accomplishes His work through you. [1]

God is at work around us and we can miss it if we are not sensitive to His voice. We need to learn to hear from God as the prophets heard from God. God says He does nothing without confirming it through His prophets. When the earth was wicked and full of sin, God called Noah, a righteous man. When Pharaoh kept God's people in bondage, God called Abraham, a faithful man. When sin overtook the world, God called Jesus, His only begotten Son to become a ransom for His lost children so we could come back into right standing with God.

When doing the research for Chapter 5, Should We Mix Politics and Religion, I had to research the word government. I found this entry on www.dictionary.com, "The act or process of governing, especially the control and administration of public policy in a political unit". God is still in control! God has control over every administration that has led the United States. He is in control of the Democrats, Republicans, Independents, Green Party and any other political party. There has to be balance and the divided parties help balance the social issues. We can be so concerned with one and not the other. We can become so consumed with the religiosity and miss God. God has control over the political unit. What are the political units of our day? The Democrats and the Republicans are the political units of our day. Do not be afraid for God is still in control.

God is calling out His people. He said *"if you confess Christ before men, He will confess you before the angels of God"* (Luke 12:8).

Jesus predicted that Peter would deny Him three times (Matthew 27:34). In Matthew 26:69-75, the events of the denial took place. Jesus knew it before hand and he predicted it. Peter said he would never be made to stumble but Jesus said He would. Jesus is still in control. He has left us the power through the Holy Spirit to accomplish His will. Proverbs 19:21 tells us *"Many are the plans in a man's heart, but it s the Lord's purpose that prevails"*. While man has many plans, God is still in control. Even if we choose not to participate in the political process, God is still in control. How many times have we seen man's plan disrupted? Everyone and everything has to come into submission of God. *"At the name of Jesus every knee will bow and every tongue will confess that Jesus is Lord"* (Philippians 2:10 – 11)! God wants to hear from us. We are to pray about all of these issues and pray for God's will to be done, not for the will of men to be done. If this political setup were to fade away today, God would still be in control. He governs the universe and He gave us this earth to govern it. He has given us all power and He has required us to pray and seek His face just as Esther had to seek His face to change her nation. If there is an issue or problem, we must first take it to God in prayer. We should then ask the Holy Spirit what our next steps are. Then we should act which is the same as exercising our faith. For James 2:20 reminds us *"faith without works is dead"*.

Christians, God is calling you! He is calling you to use your voice to speak up for righteousness. If we allow the world to overtake us, then we are not doing the work of. God has called us to be the light to a dark world. If the world was completely dark and there was one little glimpse of light out there, you could find it. If there is a little light in the world, that light can still triumph in the midst of darkness. Christian Democrat, Christian Republican, and

Christian Independent are you willing to let your little light shine? Are you willing to speak up and stand up for righteousness? Use your voice this day to spread the light, the true Gospel of Jesus Christ. Use your voice to vote for legislation that represents justice, mercy and faith. Use your voice to show the love of Christ! Get involved with what God is doing. Pray and seek God. Use your faith and put your hands to action by impacting this dark world with the love of Christ! God is still in control!

Growing Morally Questions
Do I trust God?
Will I follow Jesus example?
Do I trust the Holy Spirit to lead me into all truth?
Do I know that God is control of everything?
Will I pray as Esther did?
Will I use my voice as a vessel for Christ?

Prayer

Lord, I humble myself before You. You are the creator of heaven and earth and everything in it. You are in control of everything. You govern everything and everything has to submit to You. You left us this earth to govern it. Let us not sit idly by and let the negative influences of this world dictate how we Christians should live. You have made us the salt of the earth and many of us are loosing our flavor. Let us be a light in dark places. Let us study the scripture and be able to tell the lost why we believe what we believe. Let us pray and seek You and trust You to lead us in our all decision-making in Jesus name. Amen.

Biblical References – Moral Checkup

He who is of God hears God's words; therefore you do not hear, because you are not of God. John 8:47

Surely the Lord God does nothing, unless He reveals His secret to His servants the prophets. Amos 3:7

Many are the plans in a man's heart, but it s the Lord's purpose that prevails. Proverbs 19:21

My thoughts are not your thoughts, neither are your ways my ways. Isaiah 55:8

For the word of the LORD is right, And all His work is done in truth. Psalm 33:4

The LORD brings the counsel of the nations to nothing; He makes the plans of the peoples of no effect. Psalm 33:10

The counsel of the Lord stands forever, The plans of His heart to all generations. Psalm 33:11

But the natural man does not receive the things of the Spirit of God, for they are foolishness to him; nor can he know them, because they are spiritually discerned. But he who is spiritual judges all things, yet he himself is rightly judged by no one. 1 Corinthians 2:14-15

Freya S. Huffman

Chapter Fourteen

Can Unsaved People
Lead Us?

No man can serve two masters: for either he will hate the one, and love the other; or else he will hold to the one, and despise the other. Ye cannot serve God and mammon. Matthew 6:24

And Elijah came to all the people, and said, "How long will you falter between two opinions? If the LORD is God, follow Him; but if Baal, follow him." But the people answered him not a word. 1 Kings 18:21

Can unsaved people lead God's people? This depends on what direction your want to go. Anyone can follow a "leader" and it is your choice to follow who you want to, but when you are a Christian, you should look for people who are living out God's Word and His will. Hitler was a leader. Martin Luther King, Jr. was a leader. Bin Laden is a leader. Ministers are leaders. Donald Trump and Hillary Clinton have emerged as the leaders of the Republican and Democratic Parties respectively. We must look for leaders who exemplify the Bible and the Word of God, period. If we are to have a society based on the Word of God, we must vote for people who agree with the Word of God. We must put people in office who have a relationship with the Lord Jesus Christ on a daily basis. You may wonder why is this important. Let me explain. A person who has a relationship with Jesus Christ is one who knows and lives for Christ on a daily basis not when it is convenient. They seek God's council in their lives and they are led by the Holy Spirit. They are not afraid to speak about Christ in their daily interactions with others. Most people know from their conversation that they are a believer of the Word of God. In the first chapter and the first book of Psalms, it tells *us*

Blessed is the man who walks not in the counsel of the ungodly, nor stands in the path of sinners, nor sits in the seat of the scornful; but his delight is in the law of the Lord, and His law he meditates day and night. He shall be like a tree painted by the rivers of water, that brings forth its fruit in its season, whose leaf also shall not wither; and whatever he does shall prosper.

Now the opposite is true for the ungodly. Verse four says:

The ungodly are not so, but are like the chaff which the wind drives away. Therefore the ungodly shall not stand in the judgment, nor sinners in the congregation of the righteous. For the Lord knows the way of the righteous, but the way of the ungodly shall perish.

These scriptures alone show the consequences of following a good leader versus a poor leader. John Maxwell tells us in his leadership Bible that "as a leader we should be careful where we get our counsel. He states that a foolish leader does three things. First he or she begins to browse for the wrong counsel. Secondly he or she begins to listen to the wrong voices and lastly the leader joins the wrong inner circle". [1] We should watch who we obtain our counsel from. If they do not have a relationship with Christ and their inner circle is corrupt, then they will likely make a poor leader because their choices will send us down the wrong path. We are reminded from verse four of Psalms that the ungodly shall not stand in the judgment."

John Maxwell goes on to say that "a wise leader meditates on God's Word day and night. They meditate, examine, experience and evaluate God's word. When they receive counsel from the right inner circle, they are stable. They have inward nourishment and refreshment. They are fruitful and productive. They possess strength and durability and they are successful" (John Maxwell Leadership Bible).

There were many leaders in the Bible. John Maxwell points out that God of course was the ultimate leader. He states that after creating the universe and the planet on which we live, he handed leadership over to humankind. God created us to govern and rule. We can see this in Genesis 1:26 when God says let Us (Father, Son and Holy Spirit) make man in Our image, according to Our likeness; let him have dominion over the fish of the sea, over the birds of the air, and over the cattle, over all the earth and over creeping thing that creeps on the earth. So God created man in His own image, in the image of God He created him; male and female He created them.

He told us to be fruitful and multiply – that alone shows us that we should not have abortions which we have discussed in great detail. God has created us to govern the earth which includes the society in which we live. If we do not govern it, who will? We know that Satan is eager and ready to govern it and he is the Prince of the Air. He is using those who do not know God to accomplish his will instead of God's will. He uses us in our vote when we choose not to vote and we vote for issues that defy the Word of God. We should be careful about who we select as our leader. One party is not more superior than another.

An example of leadership is shown in the John Maxwell Leadership Bible (pg. 242).

Moses
1. Led through 40 years of desert travel

2. Was a political, diplomatic leader
3. Patiently listened to complaints
4. Led people as a peacemaking shepherd
5. Provided water form a rock when the people got thirsty

Joshua

1. Led through 30 years of conquering Canaan
2. Was a military, in-your-face leader
3. Confronted laziness and fear of the enemy
4. Led people as a tough commander

Jesus (Top Ten Leadership Principles of Jesus, Maxwell Leadership Bible, Pg. 1211)

1. Leadership is servanthood (Matthew 20:25-28;Mark 8:35).
2. Let your purpose prioritize your life (Matthew 6:33; Luke 19:10; John 17:4).
3. Live the life before you lead others (Luke 7:22, 23; John 14:11).
4. Impact comes from relationships, not positions (Luke 9:6; John 4:5-30).
5. Leaders must replenish themselves (Mark 1:35-38; 6:31).
6. Great leaders call for great commitment (Matthew 10:17; Mark 8:34-38).
7. Show security when handling tough issues (Mark 11:27-33; Luke 20:19-26).
8. Credibility comes by meeting needs and solving problems (Luke 5:12-15; 8:38,39).
9. Leaders must choose and develop their key people (Mark 3:14; Luke 10:1).
10. There is no success without a successor (Matthew 28:20; Acts 1:8). [1]

We can also look at the twelve disciples as leaders. They were all doing their own thing when Jesus came on the scene. Once they joined Christ they accepted Christ's principles.

John Maxwell says in Lessons from a lousy leader, "that leadership is not to be used for personal benefit" (Pg. 1259, Maxwell Leadership Bible).

Many think that because we are not violating the ten commandments, we are living a righteous life. We feel a little righteous and look down on others who fail in these areas. Even if we have "perfected" this area and I use this word loosely because none of us are perfect on our own, we still have to watch our hearts and motives. We can look at Luke 18:28-23. Jesus counsels the rich young ruler. Jesus always took the time to prompt change in a person.

> *Now a certain ruler asked Him, saying, "Good Teacher, what hall I do to inherit eternal life?" So Jesus said to him, "Why do you call Me good? No one is good but One, that is, God. You know the commandments: 'Do not commit adultery,' 'Do not murder,' 'Do not steal,' 'Do not bear false witness,' 'Honor your father and your mother.'" And he said, "All these things I have kept from my youth." So when Jesus heard these things, He said to him, "You still lack one thing. Sell all that you have and distribute to the poor, and you will have treasure in heaven; and come, follow Me." But when he heard this, he became very sorrowful, for he was very rich.*

Although the rich young ruler admitted that he did not violate the Ten Commandments, Jesus still had to check his heart. He had to see where his heart was. We should be able to let go of whatever God tells us to. When we cherish a material thing or possession more than we cherish God, we have made that thing our idol. This violates the second commandment, making it a god because you are worshipping it. Money does not make us evil but the Word of God says that the love of money is the root of all evil.

Ethics has long been an issue in many companies and organizations. People work hard to raise money or work for an organization to increase revenue and one bad apple can spoil an entire company. Take a look at Enron, a gas pipeline company, failed because of Ethics. Sixteen leaders of company went to prison because of unethical practices. Lobbyists approach politicians to lobby their causes but this has to be done ethically. Money is placed ahead of ethics and as a result, the people who work for the company suffer, losing their 401Ks, retirement and savings. Politicians step up to do the right thing to assist and one example is the Sarbanes-Oxley Act or SOX compliance. Senator Paul Sarbanes and Representative Michael Oxley were the architects. It was created to protect investors from fraudulent activities.

Other companies such as TyCo and WorldComm have also had questionable financial practices. These two politicians are now protecting investors by ensuring companies are signing off on financial statements that have been audited.

Not only in corporate America have there been financial scandals, there have been some in the ministry as well. Resources are needed to preach the gospel. Resources are needed to print Bibles, tracts, buy television time, start up websites, give to the poor, and build ministries. When supporters give to ministries to support the vision, it is to be used for the ministry, traveling and within the governments allowance. It should not be taken and used for frivolous things.

What Jesus was checking was His heart. He said if your eye causes you to sin, then you should pluck it out. If your hand causes you to sin, then you should cut it off. Do not go plucking out your eye or cutting off your hand! Jesus' point was, do not allow your members (the parts of your body) to cause you to sin. It is more important for your soul to be right before God than anything. Do allow the members of your body sin against God.

Can unsaved people lead Christians in a godly way? The obvious answer is no but I had to ask it because when we put people in office who do not align their votes with God's views, then we are letting unsaved people lead us. God gave us a key to set up his dominion on earth. We have the key and that key is our vote. When we vote for people out of tradition or loyalty to a party then we are taking a chance of putting unsaved people in office. When it is time to vote, we cannot be upset when the candidate votes for a law that legalizes abortion or that votes for taking prayer out of schools. We are putting unsaved people in office and we are depending on them to lead us God's way. They will not be able to.

As Christians, we are to look for those that embody our values. Voting for an unsaved leader is like allowing Satan to lead you. Seek the Holy Spirit for His guidance and look past the political party. Look at the heart as you choose the next leader.

Growing Morally Questions
Will you walk in the counsel of the ungodly?
Will you pray for Godly leadership in our government?
Will you lead like Jesus?

Prayer

Lord, You said that we should not walk in the counsel of the ungodly. We pray that You will raise up men and women of God who stand for righteousness. We pray for Your guidance in the leaders we support. We know that the candidates will not be perfect but we should seek You and allow You to guide us into the all truth. Lord You said out of the abundance of the heart the mouth speaks. Let me hear what the candidates have to say as well as watch their actions in Jesus name.

Amen.

Biblical References – Moral Checkup

No man can serve two masters: for either he will hate the one, and love the other; or else he will hold to the one, and despise the other. Ye cannot serve God and mammon. Matthew 6:24

Blessed is the man who walks not in the counsel of the ungodly, nor stands in the path of sinners, nor sits in the seat of the scornful; but his delight is in the law of the Lord, and His law he meditates day and night. He shall be like a tree painted by the rivers of water, that brings forth its fruit in its season, whose leaf also shall not wither; and whatever he does shall prosper. Psalm 1:1

Chapter Fifteen

God Can Use
a Democrat, a Republican
or an Independent!

"Be diligent to present yourself approved to God as a workman who does not need to be ashamed, accurately handling the word of truth" (2 Timothy 2:15).

Throughout history God has used many people from both parties to do His will. While we would like to proclaim our party as God's party, God can use a Democrat, Republican or Independent. We look at each other across the aisle and see the negative only but there is good on both sides. God has used many Christian Presidents and Christian leaders from the Republican and the Democratic background for good causes. The Voting Rights Act was signed into law by President Lyndon Johnson, a Democrat. President George W. Bush, has been very bold for Christ in public and is responsible for the Faith-Based Initiative. President Clinton, a Democrat, started Ameri-Corps. President Jimmy Carter, a Democrat, is a Sunday School teacher until this day and was responsible for peace efforts with many countries. He also actively participates with Habitat for Humanity. Abraham Lincoln freed the slaves.

When Jesus chose the twelve disciples they were from different backgrounds. He called them from where they were.

And when He had called His twelve disciples to Him, He gave them power over unclean spirits, to cast them out, and to heal all kinds of sickness and all kinds of disease. Now the names of the twelve apostles are these: first, Simon, who is called Peter, and Andrew his brother; James the son of Zebedee, and John his brother; Philip and Bartholomew; Thomas and Matthew the tax collector; James the son of Alphaeus, and Lebbaeus, whose surname was Thaddaeus; Simon the Cananite, and Judas Iscariot, who also betrayed Him. (Matthew 10:1-4)

Jesus used them regardless of their backgrounds. While their backgrounds were diverse, they chose to follow Christ and they accepted Him as their personal savior. They adopted His ways. They still had their issues: Judas' greed, Peter's mouth, and Matthew's tax Collecting. This holds true with many of leaders today. They have issues where they fall short in but as you look at the table below, they all have a religious affiliation.

A List of the Past and Present U.S. President's Party Affiliation and Religion 1

#	President	Party Affiliation	Religion
1	George Washington	None, Federalist	Episcopalian (Deist)
2	John Adams	Federalist	Congregationalist; Unitarian
3	Thomas Jefferson	Democratic-Republican	Episcopalian; non-denom. held Christian, Deist, Unitarian beliefs

4	James Madison	Democratic-Republican	Episcopalian (deist?)
5	James Monroe	Democratic-Republican	Episcopalian (deist?)
6	John Quincy Adams	Democratic-Republican	Unitarian
7	Andrew Jackson	Democrat	Presbyterian
8	Martin Van Buren	Democrat	Dutch Reformed
9	William Henry Harrison	Whig	Episcopalian
10	John Tyler	Whig	Episcopalian (deist)
11	James Knox Polk	Democrat	Presbyterian; Methodist
12	Zachary Taylor	Whig	Episcopalian
13	Millard Fillmore	Whig	Unitarian
14	Franklin Pierce	Democrat	Episcopalian
15	James Buchanan	Democrat	Presbyterian
16	Abraham Lincoln	Republican	Baptist; non-denomination
17	Andrew Johnson	National Union	Christian (non-denomination)
18	Ulysses S Grant	Republican	Presbyterian; Methodist
19	Rutherford B. Hayes	Republican	Presbyterian; Methodist (?)
20	James A. Garfield	Republican	Disciples of Christ

21	Chester A. Arthur	Republican	Episcopalian
22	Grover Cleveland	Democrat	Presbyterian
23	Benjamin Harrison	Republican	Presbyterian
24	Grover Cleveland	Democrat	Presbyterian
25	William McKinley	Republican	Methodist
26	Theodore Roosevelt	Republican	Dutch Reformed; Episcopalian
27	William Howard Taft	Republican	Unitarian
28	Woodrow Wilson	Democrat	Presbyterian
29	Warren G. Harding	Republican	Baptist
30	Calvin Coolidge	Republican	Congregationalist
31	Herbert Hoover	Republican	Quaker
32	Franklin Delano Roosevelt	Democrat	Episcopalian
33	Harry S. Truman	Democrat	Southern Baptist
34	Dwight D. Eisenhower	Republican	River Brethren; Jehovah's Witnesses; Presbyterian
35	John F. Kennedy	Democrat	Catholic
36	Lyndon B. Johnson	Democrat	Disciples of Christ
37	Richard M. Nixon	Republican	Quaker
38	Gerald Ford	Republican	Episcopalian
39	Jimmy Carter	Democrat	Baptist (fmr Southern

			Baptist)
40	Ronald Reagan	Republican	Disciples of Christ; Presbyterian
41	George H. W. Bush	Republican	Episcopalian
42	William Jefferson Clinton	Democrat	Baptist
43	George W. Bush	Republican	Methodist (fmr Episcopalian)
44	Barack Obama	Democratic	United Church of Christ

Taken from: (http://www.adherents.com/adh_presidents.html)
(http://www.enchantedlearning.com/history/us/pres/list.shtml)

If you are saved and you are of God, you can be used by God. You must seek God in your decision-making. This is for all men and women who hold political offices. If you are a Christian, God can use you. Your passion may be for social issues or your passion can be for moral issues, but the true Christian will have a passion for both. I really believe there is a new type of politician that will rise up today. This Christian politician will be a Proverbs man or woman. They will make wisdom the principle thing. This Christian politician will be a Spirit-filled person. They will allow the Holy Spirit to guide them in their decision-making. They will surround themselves with Godly counsel. This new politician will be like Jesus. They will care for the poor, the broken, the lost and the neglected. This Christian politician will be like Paul. They will be bold about winning souls and living a life sold out for Christ.

Is this you? Do you want to truly and fully represent the gospel or do you want to continue being unbalanced and one-sided? God is calling us back to Him. He wants us to examine our hearts and our motives. He wants to be first in our lives. He wants us to be a light to a dark world. He wants us to be fair, just and merciful. He does not want us to be hypocrites. The world is watching. They see us bashing each other. They see us neglecting each other. They see us lying to each other on each other. They see us being selfish and greedy. If we truly want to change our government, we must seek God and allow Him to use us. He will use the Christians in government to work across the aisle to get things done while everyone else is fighting. Are you ready for the challenge Christian Democrat, Christian Republican or Christian Independent? Are you ready to come together for God's work? God can use you right where you are to influence those around you!

Growing Morally Questions
Regardless of my party affiliation, will I allow God to use me just where I am?
Do I have a heart for God?
Will I become a servant of Jesus and reach out to the lost?

Prayer

Lord, I thank You for your grace and mercy. I thank You for dying on the cross for my sins. I thank You that You have washed away all my sins because I have accepted You as my personal savior. You are King of Kings and Lord of Lords. Regardless of my background, I draw nigh unto You and allow You to work through me to reach the lost, the hurting, and lead the world into the saving knowledge of Jesus Christ. In Jesus Name. Amen.

Biblical References – Moral Checkup

And when He had called His twelve disciples to Him, He gave them power over unclean spirits, to cast them out, and to heal all kinds of sickness and all kinds of disease. Now the names of the twelve apostles are these: first, Simon, who is called Peter, and Andrew his brother; James the son of Zebedee, and John his brother; Philip and Bartholomew; Thomas and Matthew the tax collector; James the son of Alphaeus, and Lebbaeus, whose surname was Thaddaeus; Simon the Cananite, and Judas Iscariot, who also betrayed Him. Matthew 10:1-5

So he sent and brought him in. Now he was ruddy, with bright eyes, and good-looking. And the LORD said, "Arise, anoint him; for this is the one!" Then Samuel took the horn of oil and anointed him in the midst of his brothers; and the Spirit of the LORD came upon David from that day forward. So Samuel arose and went to Ramah. 1 Samuel 16:12-13

Chapter Sixteen

Top Ten Moral Issues

"It will be righteousness for us if we are careful to observe all these commandments before the LORD our God, just as He commanded us" (Deuteronomy 6:25).

A moral litmus test is needed to test the candidates and their views. The moral litmus test is based on the 10 commandments and the other commandment that Jesus gave us, to love each other as Christ loved the church. Even more importantly, salvation takes precedence over all of these. If we obey the ten commandments and have not accepted Jesus as our personal savior, it does not matter anyway. We can be moral and separated from God eternally if we do not accept Jesus as our personal savior. Many think the moral litmus test is abortion only. I would say it is abortion, love, peace and everything Jesus represents. I do believe that God uses His prophets to give us direction on what He is doing at a certain time. Many of these prophets are pastors, authors and Christian leaders.

When the Pharisees asked Jesus what was the greatest commandment, He told them to love one another. Love never fails. Love never looks over a person when they are down. Love is not greedy. Love does not kill innocent babies. Love does not hurt. Love does not discriminate. Love is fair. Love is just. Love is kind. Love is gentle. Love is patient. Love is longsuffering. Love is self-control. Love is peace. Love is faithful. Love is full of joy. Love is full of goodness. These fruit of the spirit are all inside of love. This is the true litmus test.

The Ten Commandments are very important because disobeying these laws as a Christian can cause us to fall. The Bible tells us "the law is good if one uses it lawfully. The law is good if one uses it lawfully knowing this: that the law is not made for a righteous person, but for *the* lawless and insubordinate, for *the* ungodly and for sinners, for *the* unholy and profane, for murderers of fathers and murderers of mothers, for manslayers, for fornicators, for sodomites, for kidnappers, for liars, for perjurers, and if there is any other thing that is contrary to sound doctrine, according to the glorious gospel of the blessed God which was committed to my trust." **(1 Timothy 1:8-11)**

In Pastor Rod Parsley's **Silent No More**, he discusses seven topics that are controversial in today's society. This also deals with morality. According to him they are:

1. Judicial Tyranny
2. Race
3. Poverty
4. Homosexuality
5. Islam
6. Education
7. Life
8. Media

In his discussion of these topics, he effectively establishes the ground to show how we have allowed these issues to overtake this nation without the consideration of God. Even Christians are torn on these issues. In Judicial Tyranny chapter, Pastor Parsley points out how he discusses the original intent of the Constitution. In the Race chapter he discusses the fact that race is still an issue and how minorities are still not treated equal in pay or status and how Jesus embraces minorities. In the Poverty chapter he discusses the "liberal policy programs" that have led to poverty. I think we need to take care of the poor and needy and there should be a safety net to help those who do not have. I believe this should be temporary and not permanent; we cannot snatch the net from under the people but it should be gradually pulled out.

In the Islam chapter, he discusses the background of Islam and how "the God of Christianity and the god of Islam are two separate beings" (Pg 96). In the Education chapter, he discusses the education system. In the Life chapter, he discusses the abortion and planned parenthood. In the last chapter he discusses the Media and how it has no limits. Its influence is so strong on our children that they absorb everything the watch. Also, words that would make cringe are being played on family television channels without filters!

If Christians do not agree with someone's view, they should not succumb to violence. We should not bully others that do not share our beliefs. On the other hand, if someone does not agree with a Christian's view, they should not be seen as a bully or discriminated against. We should teach the word of God with compassion. We should trust God to reveal all truth. That is what true faith is, trusting God.

These issues are issues that shape the moral structure of America today. As Christians, we have the opportunity to show the world God's way. The justice system should be fair for all people and not lopsided. Race should not be an issue among Christians. Whites, African-Americans, Asians, Hispanics and Indians should be given equal consideration but this is not the case. Poverty should not be in America, the richest country on earth. Childcare, minimum wage, gas prices are all contributing factors to poverty. When you have a single mom making minimum wage with three children, it is hard to make ends meet. When you have a husband and wife who are working minimum wage, it is also hard to make it. This is where we have to witness and show people who God is. Poverty does not have to be.

As a Christian, poverty should not be in our vocabulary. God has given us principles that we can follow to become wealthy. We must show the poor love as well. We can give them fish and more importantly, teach them how to fish so they can see God move in their lives. The welfare system was a system put in place to help the poor. Many became totally dependent on this temporary system but in order to help those who are in bondage, we have to show them the way. We need to provide solutions. God is challenging us to reach back help those who do not have. Our life should be the testimony that moves them towards Christ.

Morality crosses the aisles into both parties. There are members of both political parties that have fallen short in the moral arena. Democratic and Republican leaders have made poor choices morally. God said no sin is greater and that we all have sinned. The problem is that we need to evaluate our choices. The flip side of that is that we must also forgive. Leaders are held to a higher standard and when leading a nation, a state, or community, others are watching your decision-making.

Bishop T.D. Jakes said it best when President Clinton went through his ordeal. We are missing the greatest chance to forgive. When we sin, we need to first admit the sin, repent and get it right with God. We do not need to cover it up. This is for Republicans, Democrats and Independents. We do not need to allow the Devil to keep us bound up. We need to get it right and move on. We also need to refrain from continuously beating the other person down. When a person is humbled, their spirit is broken and they are better able to receive from God but we must first repent and have a Godly sorrow. I saw this humility when Mike Brown, the FEMA Director during the Hurricane Katrina disaster, asked for forgiveness from the people. This man was broken. God can use you when you get to this level because all pride and arrogance has been stripped and now you will hear from Him. When you repent and you go through the process of restoration, your heart changes, people see this and they are more receptive of you. What is done in the dark will come out in the light for any person.

We should look for candidates who have made Christ their Lord and Savior. We should look for candidates who have a heart for God. We should look for candidates who uphold God's law and when they fall, repent and get it right with God.

Growing Morally Questions
Do I live by the Ten Commandments?
Have applied the moral litmus test to the candidates?
Will I be my brother's keeper and show them the way of God?

Prayer

Lord, your Word is true. I accept Your Word as the guide for my life. When I get off track, help me to turn back to You and humble myself. Remove anything in me that is not like You. Help me to live a life that will lead others to Christ. Never allow me to compromise the gospel but help me to share the pure, unadulterated Gospel with everyone around me.

Biblical References – Moral Checkup

The Ten Commandments

And God spoke all these words, saying: "I am the LORD your God, who brought you out of the land of Egypt, out of the house of bondage. "You shall have no other gods before Me. "You shall not make for yourself a carved image - any likeness of anything that is in heaven above, or that is in the earth beneath, or that is in the water under the earth; you shall not bow down to them nor serve them. For I, the LORD your God, am a jealous God, visiting the iniquity of the fathers upon the children to the third and fourth generations of those who hate Me, but showing mercy to thousands, to those who love Me and keep My commandments. "You shall not take the name of the LORD your God in vain, for the LORD will not hold him guiltless who takes His name in vain. "Remember the Sabbath day, to keep it holy. Six days you shall labor and do all your work, but the seventh day is the Sabbath of the LORD your God. In it you shall do no work: you, nor your son, nor your daughter, nor your male servant, nor your female servant, nor your cattle, nor your stranger who is within your gates. For in six days the LORD made the heavens and the earth, the sea, and all that is in them, and rested the seventh day. Therefore the LORD blessed the Sabbath day and hallowed it. "Honor your father and your mother, that your days may be long upon the land which the LORD your God is giving you. "You shall not murder. "You shall not commit adultery. "You shall not steal. "You shall not bear false witness against your neighbor. "You shall not covet your neighbor's house; you shall not covet your neighbor's wife, nor his male servant, nor his female servant, nor his ox, nor his donkey, nor anything that is your neighbor's." Exodus 20:1-17

"Teacher, which is the greatest commandment in the Law?" Jesus replied: " 'Love the Lord your God with all your heart and with all your soul and with all your mind. This is the first and greatest commandment. And the second is like it: 'Love your neighbor as yourself.'⁰All the Law and the Prophets hang on these two commandments." Matthew 22:36-40

Freya S. Huffman

Chapter Seventeen

The Proposition

"See, I am doing a new thing! Now it springs up; do you not perceive it? I am making a way in the wilderness and streams in the wasteland" (Isaiah 43:19).

Our country has been set up with a system of checks and balances. The Democrats and the Republicans have their own views as has been discussed in detail in this book. Many of those views do not align with the word of God however, we are forced to choose the candidate that best fits our moral and social views.

There is not a perfect candidate. In the last few elections, we have seen the flaws in our Presidential leaders. Some have created laws and that go against the moral beliefs we have. There has not been a President that has embodied all of Christs views.

As Christians, there are slim pickings! Since the choices are limited, it is time to reconsider the current political structure. There are candidates that reflect Christ's values within both political parties. The Republican Party has been promoted as the Christian party. The Democratic Party has been promoted as the socially-focused party. However, no one party **totally** exhibits Christ-like values. To say the Republican Party is a Christian party is to be deceptive. To say the Democratic Party does not have Christ-like values is also deceptive.

Does the Republican Party have Godly values? Yes, it does. Does the Democratic Party have Godly values? Yes, it does. Does the Republican Party have some flaws? Yes, it does. Does the Democratic Party have some flaws? Yes, it does.

During the presidential election of 2016, the front-runner candidates are Donald Trump (Republican) and Hillary Clinton (Democrat). This vote will be challenging if you are loyal to your political party.

I propose starting a new party! This party would focus on Christ's values which include moral and social issues. The focus would not be on one issue but on would be a culmination of many issues. There are organizations that are focusing on this today.

If you are a member of the Democratic or Republican Party and you are a Christian, vote for values that represent God. It seems the Christians are the minority however we can be majority by voting according to the word of God. Grass movements have already begun to have a Party that reflects Christs values. Now, more than ever is the time to move forward with this initiative.

It is time for action otherwise we will continue to be given the same type of choices that currently exists in the political structure. If we want change, we have to create change!

Chapter Eighteen

Your Free Gift

"For whosoever shall call upon the name of the Lord shall be saved. (Romans 10:13)

If by chance you picked up this book and you are not a Christian, this chapter is especially for you. You may have some questions and you are not sure why you would need to accept Jesus as your personal savoir. A Christian is a person who has accepted Christ as their personal savior. They have confessed with their mouth and they believe with their hearts that Jesus died on the cross for their sins. Why would you want to be a Christian you may ask?

You have an eternal soul. Our life on this earth is temporary. Even if you live to be 100 years old, your soul is eternal. When we take our last breath on this earth, we need an assurance of where our eternal soul will be. There are two choices: heaven or hell. Where do you want your eternal soul to be? According to the book of James in the Holy Bible, "our life on this earth is but a vapor".

Heaven is real and Hell is real. Your life is eternal. You have to decide if you want your soul to be eternally in Heaven or eternally in Hell. We have been given this earthly body but our soul is eternal. God gives us a free moral will to make our decisions. He does not force anyone to become a Christian. It is your choice.

Whether you believe it or not, Hell is real! There are many that are deceived will not make it to heaven because they have not accepted Christ as their personal savior. Some may ask, why do I need Jesus? How do you know this to be true? There are many reasons to know that God is real. Man did not evolve on earth and appear. Our ability to think and make our own decisions was created by God. Look at nature and all the plants, flowers, and food that we have. This did not magically appear, only a creative God could make this. Look at the weather, the sun, moon, the rain, and the earth!

Also, many religions have been created but Christianity has been stood the test of time for over 2,000 years. Christians have been martyred for their views, yet the Word of God remains and many continue to come to Christ. When we go through something tragic in life, our first call is to God. Many often say, "my God!".

While you have a free moral will, if you deny Christ, then will not make to heaven. Hell is also for those who are in a backslidden state and have not returned to Christ. The gift of salvation is free. God so loved the world that He gave His only begotten son to be a sacrifice for sinners. You alone are not good enough to enter into the Kingdom of Heaven. Jesus is the Lamb of God who came to take the sin from the world. The only way to get to heaven is through Jesus. The word of God says if you try to come any other way, you are a liar and a thief. Accept Jesus as your personal savior today. He loves you just the way you are. Do not try to get it right on your own.

You will not be good enough but when you accept Jesus as your personal savior, you are washed in the blood of Jesus and your sins are forgotten as far as the East is from the West. This is the only blood that you can be washed that will make you white as snow! God said He would take your sins and put them in the sea of forgetfulness. Will you accept this gift today? Will you accept Jesus as your Lord and personal savior? Will you make Him Lord over your life? You will spend eternity with Him where you will be perfect before God.

Once you have said this sinner's prayer, rejoice because you have been reconciled to Christ! You get the benefits of being the King's child. The angels in heaven are rejoicing for you this day. You even have angels assigned to you now, praise God. God loves you and He has been waiting for you. Get in a Bible-believing church and study the Word of God so you have the tools needed to live a successful Christian life. Fellowship with other Christian brothers and sisters so you can continue to grow in Christ.

A Sinner's Prayer

Lord, I acknowledge that I am a sinner. I ask that your will forgive me of my sins. I believe in my heart and confess with my mouth that Jesus is the Son of God. I believe that He died on the cross for my sins and He was raised from the dead in three days. I repent and turn away from my sins. I will follow after you all the days of my life. I give my life to you in Jesus name.

Amen.

Biblical References – Moral Checkup

As it is written, there is none righteous, no, not one. Romans 3:10

For all have sinned, and come short of the glory of God. Romans 3:23

Wherefore, as by one man sin entered into the world, and death by sin, and so death passed upon all men, for that have sinned. Romans 5:12

For the wages of sins death, but the gift of God is eternal life through Jesus Christ our Lord. Romans 6:23

But God commended his love toward us, in that, while we were yet sinners Christ died for us. Romans 5:8

That if thou shalt confess with thy mouth the Lord Jesus, and shalt believe in thine heat that God has raised him from the dead, thou shalt be saved. For with the heart man believeth unto righteousness; and with the mouth confession is made unto salvation. For the scripture saith, Whosoever believeth on him shall not be ashamed. Romans 10:9-11

Come unto me, all ye labour and are heavy laden, and I will give you rest. Take my yoke upon you, and learn of me; for I am meek and lowly in heart: and ye shall find rest unto your souls. Matthew 11:28-29

All that the Father giveth shall come to me; and him that cometh to me I will in no wise cast out. John 6:37

For by grace are you saved through faith and that not of yourselves: it is the gift of God: Not of works, lest any man should boast. Ephesians 2:8-9

Scriptural references taken from Antioch Baptist Church Tract, Harlem Georgia

Conclusion

Are God's People Revolving or Evolving?

"but grow in the grace and knowledge of our Lord and Savior Jesus Christ To Him be the glory, both now and to the day of eternity. Amen." (2 Peter 3:8)

When something revolves, it goes around the same axis or rotation continuously. When something evolves, it is changed or transformed. The evolution I am speaking of is not Darwinism. I am speaking evolving or being made into the image of Christ. Genesis tells us that God created man in His image. Romans 12:12 tells us "do not be conformed to this world, but be ye transformed by the renewing of your mind, that you may prove what is that good and acceptable and perfect will of God". 2 Corinthians tells us that "we are being transformed into the same image from glory to glory, just as by the Spirit of the Lord".

We should also have the mind of Christ. We should consider how Christ would respond to issues on earth today. We should mirror Christ's way of handling issues and we should pray and seek God before we make any decisions. We must make our allegiance to Christ before man, race, gender or a political party. We should continue to evolve into the image Christ. This can be accomplished through prayer and meditation in the word of God. Seek God. Trust the Holy Spirit's guidance and He will lead you into all truth. No matter what any political party says, the final word is always Jesus. No matter what law passes, what party wins, or disaster happens, God is always in control. Are you ready to trust Him and seek Him? Are you ready to be transformed into who He has called you to be? Become the evolving, transforming people that Christ has called you to be. Use Christ's example and reach everyone with His word and by showing His love to all. This is the only way Christians will truly impact the world with their vote!

Powerful Quotes

What should be the uppermost in the minds of Christian voters as they go to the polls on Tuesday? What is the real meaning of patriotic responsibility for Christians in the often very worldly business of American politics? Our first call is not an allegiance of party; it is not an allegiance of personal interest; it is not an allegiance to social good. Our first call is to God Almighty. And at the expense of all things, we must serve that allegiance – for that is what Our Lord did and that is what, by His example, we are called to do.

-Alan Keyes

John F. Kennedy On Liberalism... "...liberalism is our best and only hope in the world today. For the liberal society is a free society, and it is at the same time and for that reason a strong society. Its strength is drawn from the will of free people committed to great ends and peacefully striving to meet them. Only liberalism, in short, can repair our national power, restore our national purpose, and liberate our national energies. What do our opponents mean when they apply to us the label 'Liberal?' If by 'Liberal' they mean, as they want people to believe, someone who is soft in his policies abroad, who is against local government, and who is unconcerned with the taxpayer's dollar, then the record of this party and its members demonstrate that we are not that kind of "Liberal."

But if by a "Liberal" they mean someone who looks ahead and not behind, someone who welcomes new ideas without rigid reactions, someone who cares about the welfare of the people -- their health, their housing, their schools, their jobs, their civil rights, and their civil liberties -- someone who believes we can break through the stalemate and suspicions that grip us in our policies abroad, if that is what they mean by a 'Liberal,' then I am proud to say I am a 'Liberal.'"

-President John F. Kennedy
http://www.liberalslikechrist.org/politicalmenu.htm

"If Jesus of Nazareth was <u>anything</u>, he was an extraordinary friend of the downtrodden, definitely a Liberal, whose advocacy on their behalf so infuriated the ultra-Conservative religious and political leaders of his day that they had him killed to prevent the public from hearing the very <u>liberal</u> teaching that you will see quoted <u>in Jesus' own words</u>" www.liberalsforchrist.org

-Elias Boudinot: | Portrait of Elias Boudinot

"Be religiously careful in our choice of all public officers . . . and judge of the tree by its fruits."

http://www.eadshome.com/QuotesoftheFounders.htm

"God governs in the affairs of man. And if a sparrow cannot fall to the ground without his notice, is it probable that an empire can rise without His aid? We

have been assured in the Sacred Writings that except the Lord build the house, they labor in vain that build it. I firmly believe this. I also believe that, without His concurring aid, we shall succeed in this political building no better than the builders of Babel" – Constitutional Convention of 1787 | original manuscript of this speech

-Benjamin Franklin: | Portrait of Ben Franklin

http://www.eadshome.com/QuotesoftheFounders.htm

"I'M A DEMOCRAT BECAUSE when I was growing up in Alabama, black men and women weren't allowed to even register to vote. They almost gave up. I think about the next generation, and I don't want to give up. There's still work to be done. I want to stand with the party that fights for everyone."

-Representative John Lewis

http://www.democrats.org/

Freya S. Huffman

VOTING GUIDELINE

This is not an inclusive guideline. It is intended to give Christians a basic guideline to follow when selecting candidates. Even after answering these questions, it is still the Christians responsibility to seek God and pray before they cast their vote.

o Does the candidate believe in the Lord Jesus Christ as his personal savior? (Salvation)

o Does the candidate believe in the Ten Commandments? (Faithfulness)

o Does the candidate believe in equal treatment of all people? (Justice)

o Does the candidate believe in supporting the poor and needy? (Mercy)

o Does the candidate support prayer in schools? (Acknowledging God)

o Does the candidate love all people? (Love)

o Is the candidate saved?

o Does the candidate believe in justice, mercy and faithfulness?

o Does the candidate's actions align with the word of God in word and in deed?

o Does the candidate support ten commandments in schools?

o Is the candidate in support of the marriage of a man and woman?

o Is the candidate against abortion?

o Does the candidate tell the truth?

o Does the candidate believe in equal treatment of all people?

o Is the candidate concerned about social issues such as poverty, social security, Medicare, health, sickness, and support of third-world countries?

Helpful Links

http://www.ontheissues.org

http://www.wallbuilders.org

http://www.liberalslikechrist.org/

http://www.humaneventsonline.com/

http://www.justiceatthegate.org/

www.leadlikejesus.com

http://www.keyway.ca/htm2002/whydoit.htm

http://www.masscouncilofchurches.org/docs/doc_affirmative.htm

http://rac.org/advocacy/issues/issueaa/

http://nursepat.com/black.html

http://www.godspolitics.com

http://www.presidentialprayer.com

http://www.centerformoralclarity.net/

http://www.declareyourself.org/ - Register to Vote

http://www.eadshome.com/QuotesoftheFounders.htm

What Does the Bible Say About Voting?
http://bible.com/bibleanswers_result.php?id=237

http://www.generals.org/index.php?id=1591

President Obama's Beliefs
http://www.wanttoknow.info/008/obama_religious_beliefs_views

Christian Democrats of America
http://www.christiandemocratsofamerica.org/about-us/what-is-cdoa/

Prayer for the Nation
by Freya S. Huffman

For the kingdom of God is the Lord's and rules over all nations. Psalm 22:28

Lord in the mighty and matchless name of Jesus, I exalt You this day. This is the day that You have made and we will rejoice in it. You are holy, mighty, righteous, loving, just and faithful. Lord, God we pray for this nation, the United States of America, to turn her heart back to You. Lord, God this nation was founded on Christian principles and was built on the word of God. Lord You brought us into Your light.

Lord we repent for this nation because we have turned our backs on You. You left us a blueprint, the Bible, to follow and we have allowed ungodly legislation to enter law books to govern us. We have voted for causes that totally contradict Your word and we have neglected to vote. Lord, for this we apologize.

We apologize for neglecting the poor and the needy and putting our own selfish desires for power and authority before the care of Your people. Lord we repent for allowing the Ten Commandments and Prayer to be taken out of the schools. Lord we repent for not teaching our children Your word and Your ways. Lord we repent for pushing our own agenda ahead of Your agenda. We repent for not using our rights to vote men and women in office who reflect Your Word. Forgive us for being unbalanced. Forgive us for misrepresenting the Christian faith and for being hypocrites. Lord, unsaved people are watching us and they see hypocrisy and deceit. Lord, help us to learn to work together to accomplish the greater good for this country.

Lord we come against all ungodly legislation in Jesus name. We come against lobbyists who commit their time and money to lobby against the Word of God. We pray that no weapon formed against your people shall prosper and that Your law will override any law that is created on earth.

We pray that You will touch the heart of the President, Presidential Cabinet Members, Senators, Congressmen, Congresswomen, State Representative, Oval Office members, Governors, Mayors, City Council Man and City Council Woman that they will desire to do Your will and vote Your values. We pray for righteous authority. You said in Your word that when the righteous are in the authority, the people rejoice. We pray for righteous leaders to step forth. We pray for unity in the cabinet and the willingness and desire to work across party lines.

We come against any leaders that would try to stand against Your word. We pray that they will not prevail.

We come against terrorists and extremist that hate America. We pray that they will not prevail. We pray You uncover every terrorist cell and the enemy will not prevail. We pray You will touch the hearts of enemies so they will come into the light of Jesus. We pray they will learn about the love of Jesus and His desire to see all men saved and that no man will perish.

We pray for our spiritual leaders: Apostles, Pastors, Prophets, Evangelists, and Teachers to teach and preach Your word with authority and love. We pray they will seek Your face and hear Your voice during this hour. We pray they will share Your word with Your people and direct Your people in the right direction. Give Your people increased spiritual discernment. Let us not be fooled by the words of man but give us discernment to see their true fruits.

I come against prejudice, racism, sexism, and ageism. Lord You said You have no respect of a person and that You will use anyone that You want to use. I pray for unity in the church. I pray that Your people will work together to reach lost souls for Jesus Christ. I also pray that Your people will seek Your face and turn back to You.

I pray that You will give our legislatures wisdom and sensitivity to the needs of Your people. I pray that You will expose every corrupt and lying spirit. I pray that You will guide us as we vote on election day. You said Your people perish because of lack of knowledge. Help us to do our homework on each candidate. Help us to seek Your face in prayer and fasting to see what is best for this nation. Give us the boldness to act on what You speak to us.

We come against ungodly legislation and ungodly bills. We pray the lobbyists are quitting. They will not lobby against your word but for your word. Give them a change of heart in Jesus name.

We bind deception in Jesus' name that your people are not deceived by words. Let your kingdom come and your will be done in Jesus name. We come against the spirit of hate that is against America. We speak healing for our land and come against violence in the United States. Lord we come against poverty, sickness and diseases.

Lord, we pray for our troop's safety and protection. We pray that you expose every terrorist cell and every enemy that would try to harm the United States of America. We push back the hand of the enemy and dispatch Your angels to every member of our armed forces and pray they are covered in the blood of Jesus. We pray they will have the right equipment to fight this war. We pray that we will be able to bring them home soon. We thank You for their sacrifice for our freedom and our country. Forgive us for not standing in the gap for them. Forgive us for being critical when we should be prayerful. Thank You for the freedom that You have given this country. Give the leaders of our armed forces wisdom and guidance. We pray for peace among all nations. We pray that salvation will take place in foreign lands.

We pray You will give the Central Intelligence Agency Your Intelligence which supersedes anything we can think of. Give them inside knowledge so they can stop the enemy in the planning stages. Give the Federal Bureau of Investigation Your insight to stop terrorists who would try to hurt innocent people of this nation. We pray for law enforcement to be fair and just in all of their dealings. We come against racial profiling in Jesus name. We pray for sound and just investigations in Jesus name. We pray for righteous people to enter law enforcement and the government. Remove every person from these decision-making positions whose heart is far from You in Jesus name.

Lord, we ask that You give our President wisdom and guidance in his decision-making. Give him a heart for all people. Give him wisdom to work across party lines. Give him wisdom to lead and guide Your people. Give him a heart to help the homeless, elderly, poor, needy, sick, fatherless, motherless, uneducated, teenagers, veterans, minorities, and majorities. We also pray for healthcare for those who cannot afford it and preventive programs to help our society become healthier. Put the right people in his path. Uproot every person whose motives are impure. Let him not be deceived by familiar spirits but let him test every person to see if they are of God.

Give us wisdom for the upcoming election. Lead us in our vote. Let us seek Your face and vote righteously. Give us balance and understanding of what You are doing at this hour. Let us stay away from party lines and vote according to the Word of God. Let us not be deceived by leaders who have their own agenda. Lord allow Your Holy Spirit to lead us into all truth in Jesus name.

Lord, we give this nation back to You. We pray that You will tear down everything that would exalt itself against Your word.

We pray for mercy on the United States of America. We pray that we will turn our hearts back to You and that we will vote prayer and the Ten Commandments back into the school system. We give our school system back to You. We come against crime, premature death, fights and bomb threats. We pray that school leaders will see the importance of having Christ in school. We pray You will touch the hearts of the decision-makers and they will turn their hearts to You in Jesus name.

We declare and decree that the United States of America is Your country and it belongs to You. We give it back to You. Help us to use our God-given authority to do Your will in Jesus name.

Amen.

Freya S. Huffman

Prayer Targets

1. Pray for the President
2. Pray for the Congress
3. Pray for the Senate
4. Pray for the National Government
5. Pray for the State Government
6. Pray for the Local Government
7. Pray for the children
8. Pray for the elderly
9. Pray for veterans
10. Pray against terrorism
11. Pray for deliverance from lesbianism and homosexuality
12. Pray for unity in the church and government
13. Pray for divine protection
14. Pray for blessings
15. Pray for curses to be broken
16. Pray for Forgiveness
17. Pray for God's will to be done
18. Pray for the poor and neglected
19. Pray for the abused
20. Pray for Pastors and Ministers
21. Pray for schools
22. Pray for Israel
23. Pray against crime
24. Pray against racism and prejudice
25. Pray for businesses (large and small)
26. Pray against debt
27. Pray for the military
28. Pray for the lost
29. Pray for families that have lost loved ones

30. Pray for the prison system
31. Pray for the homeless
32. Pray for the fatherless and the motherless
33. Pray for Hollywood
34. Pray for Athletes
35. Pray for music artists
36. Pray for the family (marriages kept together and broken marriages restored)
37. Pray for the sick
38. Pray for the jobless
39. Pray against divorce
40. Pray against abortion
41. Pray for judges (Federal, State, and Local) justice and mercy
42. Pray for prayer in school
43. Pray for the 10 commandments to be put up in public places
44. Pray for the Media (all media is fair and balanced on all sides)

Resources

Chapter 2

1. Mark May. "What Does the Bible Say Is Important to God". December 1997. 2005. http://www.lilacway.com/lessons/importnt.php.

2. Got Questions.org. "Does the Bible Teach that Life Begins at Conception" 2006. www.gotquestions.org/life-begin-conception.html, God Questions.org

3. http://www.bible.com/bibleanswers_result.php?id=211

4. National Right to Life Committee. "When Does Life Begin" 2006. www.nrlc.org/abortion/wdlb/wdlb.html.

www.bible1.crosswalk.com/Concordances/NavesTopicalBible/ntb.cgi?number=T78, Crosswalk, 2006

Chapter 3

1. Lea, Thomas and Hudson, Tom. **Step by Step of the New Testament.** Lifeway Church Resources

2. **Wayne Black.** "Who Were the Pharisees?" The Church of God Daily Bible Study. 2006. http://www.keyway.ca/htm2002/pharisee.htm.

Chapter 4

1. www.dictionary.com

Chapter 5

1. "Where Did the Phrase Separation of Church and State Originate?" 2005. http://members.tripod.com/~candst/tnppage/who2.htm.

2. **David Barton.** "Separation of Church and State". Wallbuilders. 2004. http://www.wallbuilders.org.

3. http://www.thetruthinblackandwhite.com/_upload/HILC_USAT_FINAL_ARL.pdf

4. **World Net Daily.** "Christian Leaders Urge the 'Biblical' Vote. 2004. http://worldnetdaily.com/news/article.asp?ARTICLE_ID=40836

5. **Bynum, Juanita.** Matters of the Heart. Charisma House

Chapter 6

1. "Christian Votes". 2006. http://www.www.christianvotes.com/templates/cuschristianvotes/details.asp?id=27567&PID=162621.

Chapter 8

1. Liberals Like Christ. 2006 http://www.liberalslikechrist.org/politicalmenu.htm.

2. www.dictionary.com

3. The Democratic Party, 2006 http://www.democrat.org

Chapter 9

1. www.dictionary.com

2. "Ten Worst Government Programs". Human Events Online. 2006. www.humaneventsonline.com/article.php?id=3209.

Chapter 10

1. **MSN Encarta.** "Democratic Party". 2005. http://encarta.msn.com/encyclopedia_761561572_2/Democratic_Party.html.

2. **MSN Encarta.** "Republican Party". 2005. http://ca.encarta.msn.com/encyclopedia_761568416_1/Republican_Party.html.

3. "Democrats vs. Republicans: What Do They Believe?". On the Issues. 2004 www.ontheissues.org/askme/dem_rep.htm.

4. "Maps and cartograms of the 2004 US presidential election results." 2006 http://www-personal.umich.edu/~mejn/election/

5. Lea, Thomas and Hudson, Tom. **Step by Step of the New Testament.** Lifeway Church Resources

6. The Associated Press. "Truth About Issues." 2005 www.truthout.org/cgi-bin/artman/exec/view.cgi/37/10925.

Chapter 11

1. King, Claude and Blackaby, Henry. **Experiencing God.** Lifeway Church Resources

Chapter 12

1. http://www.csusm.edu/Black_Excellence/documents/pg-r-reconstruction.html

2. http://seattlepi.nwsource.com/opinion/135075_oscareason15.html

3. http://www.ohiogop.org/Outreach.aspx?ID=5

4. http://www.mecca.org/~crights/dream.html

5. Weeks III, Thomas. **Even As Your Soul Prospers.** Harrison House, 2004.

Chapter 13

1. King, Claude and Blackaby, Henry. **Experiencing God.** Lifeway Church Resources www.dictionary.com

2. "Christian Votes". 2006. www.christianvotes.com/templates/cuschristianvotes/details.asp?id=27567&PID=163360.

Chapter 14

1. Maxwell, John. **Maxwell Leadership Bible**. Thomas Nelson, 2002.

Chapter 15

1. "Religious Affiliation of the U. S. Presidents". Adherents.com. 2004 www.adherents.com/adh_presidents.html.

2. Enchanted Learning. "The Presidents of the United States." 2004 www.enchantedlearning.com/history/us/pres/list.shtml.

Chapter 16

1. "What Does the Bible Say About Abortion." 2005. http://www.bible.com/bibleanswers_result.php?id=211.

2. Parsley, Rod. **Silent No More**. Charisma House, 2006.

For preaching and teaching engagements, contact Pastor Rod P. Huffman and Freya Sullivan Huffman at rhemi@outlook.com and freyamotivates@gmail.com

Freya S. Huffman

WAYNESBORO DELIVERANCE EVANGELISTIC CHURCH
SUMMER REVIVAL
THEME: EMPOWERED TO PURSUE! (1 SAMUEL 30:8)

REVIVAL
FIRE

HOSTS
Pastor Glenn Wiggins, Sr.
Co-Pastor Betty Wiggins

DATES:
JUNE 1ST - JUNE 3RD
WEDNESDAY - FRIDAY
7 PM NIGHTLY

- Deliverance!
- Salvation!
- Breakthrough!

Pastor Rod P. Huffman is an International Evangelist and Church Planter from Montgomery, Alabama. He is the founder of New Destiny Community Church (Cocoa, Florida) and Rod Huffman Evangelistic Ministries International (RHEMI). He was licensed to preach the glorious gospel in 1995 and later ordained in 1998. Pastor Huffman has spread the gospel for 21 years in three continents and seven countries including Canada, Kuwait, Saudi Arabia, Ireland, Italy, South Korea and the U.S.

He is a 20 year military veteran of the U.S. Air Force and serves as a Senior Master Sargeant.

He resides in Warner Robins, Georgia with his wife, Freya Sullivan Huffman, along with their children.

938 Old Millen Highway
Waynesboro, GA 30830
(706) 554-7338

Contact Administrator Norma Carswell
for more information.

Freya Huffman is available for speaking engagements and public appearances. For more information contact:

Freya Huffman
C/O Advantage Books
P.O. Box 160847
Altamonte Springs, FL 32716
info@ advbooks.com

To purchase additional copies of this book or other books published by Advantage Books call our order number at:

407-788-3110 (Book Orders Only)

or visit our bookstore website at:
www.advbookstore.com

Longwood, Florida, USA
"we bring dreams to life"™
www.advbookstore.com